Hidden Gems

**Naming and Teaching from the Brilliance
in Every Student's Writing**

KATHERINE BOMER

HEINEMANN
PORTSMOUTH, NH

Heinemann

361 Hanover Street

Portsmouth, NH 03801–3912

www.heinemann.com

Offices and agents throughout the world

The author and publisher wish to thank those who have generously given permission to reprint borrowed material:

"The Thing You Must Remember" from *Windfall: New and Selected Poems* by Maggie Anderson. Copyright © 2000 by Maggie Anderson. Published by the University of Pittsburgh Press. Reprinted by permission of the publisher.

Library of Congress Cataloging-in-Publication Data

Bomer, Katherine.

  Hidden gems : naming and teaching from the brilliance in every student's writing / Katherine Bomer.

      p. cm.

  Includes bibliographical references and index.

  ISBN-13: 978-0-325-02965-8

  ISBN-10: 0-325-02965-2

1. English language—Composition and exercises—Study and teaching.   2. Motivation in education.   I. Title.

  LB1576.B514 2010

  808'.042071—dc22

                                                     2010000270

Editor: Kate Montgomery

Production management: DB Publishing Services, Inc.

Production coordinator: Vicki Kasabian

Cover design: Lisa A. Fowler

Photograph on cover: Jewels © Comstock/Corbis

Author photograph: Kenneth Hipkins

Typesetter: House of Equations, Inc.

Manufacturing: Steve Bernier

Printed in the United States of America on acid-free paper

20 19 18 17 16 VP 3 4 5 6

Contents

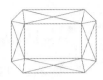

The Thing You Must Remember

The thing you must remember is how, as a child,
you worked hours in the art room, the teacher's
hands over yours, molding the little clay dog.
You must remember how nothing mattered
but the imagined dog's fur, the shape of his ears
and his paws. The gray clay felt dangerous,
your small hands were pressing what you couldn't
say with your limited words. When the dog's back
stiffened, then cracked to white shards
in the kiln, you learned how the beautiful
suffers from too much attention, how clumsy
a single vision can grow, and fragile
with trying too hard. The thing you must
remember is the art teacher's capable
hands: large, rough and grainy,
over yours, holding on.

—*Maggie Anderson*

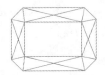

Acknowledgments

I wish to thank all the students whose writing voices sing on these pages. Their honest, sweet, and funny words lift me and stagger me and make me want to live amongst children in classrooms for the rest of my life.

Hundreds of teachers in schools around the country and in my Teachers College Reading and Writing summer institute courses over the past several years bravely tried on this work of reading student writing like artists; they are the true hidden gems of the earth, shining their intelligent voices and open hearts throughout this book. I am grateful to Sindy Maxwell, Liz Roberts, Sandy Schillperoot, literacy coaches, principals, and teachers from Sunnyside School District, Washington State; Mary Dentrone, literacy coach, Anthony Inzerillo, principal, and teachers from PS 199 in Queens, New York; Andrea Evert, literacy coach, Anne-Marie Scalfaro, principal, and teachers at PS 68 in Queens, New York; Jen Jeffries and Jennifer Logan, literacy coaches, Jack Spatola, principal, and teachers at PS 172 in Brooklyn, New York; Debbie Walton, literacy coach, Stephanie McBride, former principal, and teachers from Greene Elementary, Clear Creek Independent School District, Texas; and Laura Adlis and Diane Newmann, literacy coaches, Debbie Phillips, former principal, and teachers from Stewart Elementary, Clear Creek ISD. These groups in particular hosted several sessions of reading student writing accompanied by much joyful laughing, crying, and new language to name its brilliance. Alyssa Toomes, literacy coach, Kathy Gouger, principal, and teachers at Ward Elementary, Clear Creek ISD also read an early draft of Chapter 1 of my book and gave me inspiration to keep writing, precisely when I needed it.

More than forty teachers from all over the country quickly and enthusiastically sent samples of their students' writing when I put out an all-points-bulletin email message asking for help. It was truly impossible to choose which pieces to include in this book. I want teachers to know that all of the writing they sent was fantastic, and I will keep it in my treasure file of kids' work. This book would have been impossible to write, obviously, without the delightful pieces that I did choose—sent by their giving teachers and literacy coaches, who sometimes chased after permission letters through several address changes going back a few years. Thank you all so much: Jonathan Babcock, Melanie Bukartek, Barbara Clements, Julieanne Harmatz, Evi Hickman, Heather Hughes, Tracy Hunter, Betsy Kelly, Deb Kelt, Jennifer Kesler, Sindy Maxwell, Kristal Nichols, Bill Ryan, Regina Stone, Amber Boyd Vincent, and Sharon Woods.

Lucy Calkins generously invited me to teach several advanced summer institute sections at the Teachers College Reading and Writing Project to experiment with ideas that became the content of this book. Lucy's stunning first book, *Lessons from a Child*, enlightened me over twenty years ago, when I was a newling at the Project, about how kids have writing processes and strokes of genius in their texts when given time and encouragement to do so.

Peter Johnston's book *Choice Words* made a tremendous impact on my thinking about the language teachers use to influence students' learning and agency in a democratic classroom community. I think his book should be required reading for anyone responsible for the minds and hearts of children.

Kate Montgomery, the dearest and brightest editor, read my nascent manuscript, especially the chapter about grading, the way I wish the whole world would read student work—believing meaning hides in there somewhere. She noticed specific phrases she liked, named places where my writing moved her, and made stunning suggestions for improving the book.

The editorial and production team at Heinemann waited a long time for this book and then worked way too close to the last minute for me, especially Vicki Kasabian, in whose enormously capable hands I would leave anything of value, and Olivia MacDonald, who one day fielded, I counted, fourteen email pleas for her help and guidance. I turned my final draft over to Denise Botelho, my project manager and copy editor, for her online edits of my errors, which she blessedly did not count or grade. She smoothed out all the rough edges and did it with professional kindness.

Randy Bomer, my husband and most-trusted colleague, fed me articles and books by language education researchers and theorists so that I could fit my ideas and opinions into important ongoing conversations about responding to student work. At any moment Randy would stop and talk about my writing with me, never flagging in his interest, despite the project extending well beyond the intended end point. He read parts of the book like the artist that he is, finding more in the words than was there, and he gave shrewd advice and specific, nitty-gritty help on many impossible tasks. As if all of that weren't enough, he nurtured me with exquisite dinners every night, served with love.

Hidden Gems

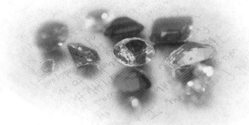

What If We Just Relaxed and Stopped Caring What the Neighbors Think?

If you're going to teach him how to write, first you have to love him.
If you can convince him of that, there's nothing you can't teach him.
—AVI

I grew up in a modest neighborhood in what was, in the early 1960s, the very northeast edge of Albuquerque, New Mexico. Our house represented one of the four building model options available in this section. I made a game of walking the streets forming the grid of this planned subdivision to find all the houses that matched ours exactly, window-for-window; and the builders couldn't trick me by reversing the plan, by making the garage on the left side of the kitchen, for instance, instead of the right. Blessedly, my own house escaped total, rigid conformity by its lucky placement on a slightly larger corner lot, atop a gentle elevation, and by having a cool driveway crossing the entire front yard, with egress on two different streets. Neighborhood kids loved to roller-skate, skateboard, and ride their bikes on this little concrete slope, and teenagers loved to drive across it, saving themselves the trouble of turning the corner the normal way.

But there were clusters of houses in the south and northwest valleys, and in little, centuries-old villages on the outskirts of Albuquerque that fascinated me with their diverse appearances. The roads were dirt. Many houses sat on at least an acre of land and were working farms, raising horses, goats, and chickens, as well as corn, beans, and chile peppers. The *casas* (houses) were built of mud and straw *adobe* bricks, with flat roofs, and they sat lower to the ground than houses in my subdivision. They looked as if they had grown straight up from the dirt, in colors ranging from tan to terra cotta.

To many visiting these regions for the first time, the preponderance of brown mud houses with dirt yards—of houses built without pitched roofs, sidewalks, well-kept lawns and shrubs pruned into geometric shapes—might have appeared disheveled and haphazard, compared with the squared-off neighborhoods in the expanding city. These houses seemed to sprawl and spread on a whim, each with a unique shape and personality, and it proved impossible to judge, unlike in the carefully prescribed suburbs of the city, who might have tremendous amounts of money, and who might not.

I thought these old village sites were beautiful. I loved that each handmade house was different and each seemed to be situated on the land according to sunrises and sunsets, or to sources of some private inspiration, their faces turned east toward the stately mountains or west toward the cozy, intimate Rio Grande River Valley. The front door might be found on any side of the house. Mostly, I admired how the human-made (both women and men contributed to house building) structures blended into and reflected the natural New Mexican landscape of desert and mountains. At sunset, the eye could sweep across homes and farms as if they were simply great swaths of earth dotted with wildflowers, toward the magenta Sandia Mountains.

When I was in college at the University of New Mexico, I chose to live in the Northwest Valley area of Albuquerque, in a tiny adobe *casita* (which was actually a converted garage) behind a not much larger main house. I inherited a little garden with peach trees, hollyhocks, roses, and chile peppers growing in abundance and without elaborate plan or boundaries, and certainly without a moment of attention from my young-adult self. I could see the Sandia Mountains from my windows; I could park my old, dented Toyota Corolla in front of the house without shame; I could let my puppy race around the land surrounding the house, tumbling about with dozens of other dogs, without worrying about the neighbors' wrath; I could meet my fellow valley dwellers, who were professors, artists, musicians, mixed in with families who had lived in this same spot for hundreds of years, and still spoke Spanish and made fresh tortillas and beans daily. I could practice speaking Spanish and not worry about making a bad grade for my mistakes. This community folded me in, without judgment or derision. My mother's worried refrain: "What will the neighbors think?" did not apply in this place because my neighbors were at least as unconventional as I was. I felt at home for the first time in my life.

Accepting Diversity in Young Persons' Ways with Words

So what, you should be asking by now, does this have to do with looking at the writing of eight- to fifteen-year-olds?

I think that the New Mexican landscape I grew up in, with its mixed languages and communities, helped shape my identity and my worldview. I am happiest with policies and practices that include everyone and miserable with too many constrictions, rules and prejudices, or any kind of practices that might belittle someone who does not conform to elitist conventions about what is considered valuable or correct.

As a writer and a reader, I am happiest with surprising, fresh ways of using language and shaping texts. I am uncomfortable when language is forced to fit into formulas determined by notions of correctness and acceptability in school settings and does not reflect how people writing outside of schools use language and genre to convince and move readers, to open eyes, to discover through the act of writing, or to express beauty and deep emotion.

This does not mean that I think spelling "doesn't count," or that I don't respect grammar, the architecture of language. It does not mean that I think writing should look like the ramblings of a mad diarist and never find the grace and power of genre or sentence boundaries. On the contrary, I am grammar's biggest fan. I admire sonnets and classic text forms. I love well-researched nonfiction, and I certainly love clear instructions for how to use my cell phone or put together a desk from IKEA. But I also value writing that breaks the conventions of what is "good" and "bad" to do in writing; I value young people's "ways with words" (Heath 1983) that are pertinent to their languages and communities, and I despise grading, testing, or instruction that forces young writers to produce texts similar to prefabricated homes with shrubs pruned into uniform balls, when what kids are writing comes from their precisely unconventional minds and hearts naming the world in new and unusual ways.

Certainly, as teachers, we want to help our students grow as writers. We want to help them recognize and become fluent with a variety of text forms, codes of convention, or as Lisa Delpit (1995) calls it, the "Edited English" that our culture has created and agreed upon in order to communicate with one another. We truly want the best for our student writers, and we do not want them to be judged for any perceived lack of intelligence about "correctness" in writing. With the barrage of benchmarks and standardized tests resulting from federal legislation called No Child Left Behind, we feel even greater pressure to help children perform well on writing tasks. We even worry over their college admission essays that allow them to gain entrance to schools of their choice. We are given many hoops to jump through these days, and although the hoops are predictable and rather low to the ground, we still labor over how to help students score as many points as possible before we turn them over to the next level of performance standards.

Teachers rightly wonder how to help kids approach any new writing task with ease and fluency, with clear thinking and organizing tools, and with a writing style that will help their pieces stand out from the other prefab essays. (Remember the cool driveway on my otherwise unimaginative house model number four in Albuquerque?)

We have come to believe that strong lessons demonstrating aspects of the writing process, style, and genre features, and writing conferences focused on individuals' writing issues will help kids improve dramatically because we've seen the evidence in their work. Yet teachers often tell me that they stumble over things to say in minilessons and conferences, particularly how to notice and name positive aspects in every student's writing, and how to teach beyond language conventions or organization of school genres such as the infamous five-paragraph essay. Because of our own highly standardized writing backgrounds in middle school, high school, and even college, we all share lenses for looking at student writing that include spelling, grammar, punctuation, and organization rules. Some of us were evaluated with rubrics in school and accept them as a more just and much clearer process for sorting pieces of writing into "proficient" or "low-performing." However, the world of writing is vastly richer than a list of spelling words or grammar rules or even the boxes provided on rubrics, and what we need is a full array of lenses for reading student writing. We can notice when students play with time and order of events in an unusual way, or when they manage to empathize with a person of the opposite gender or from another period in history so that they can create that person's inner life in a believable way. We can recognize that our students' writing reflects diverse and evolving cultures, with influences from multiple languages and visual and digital literacies.

> What we need is a full array of lenses for reading student writing.

We can also celebrate student writing by appreciating how often its odd syntax mirrors modern texts, especially the literature of some of the twentieth century's most famous writers in the English language, such as Gertrude Stein, Samuel Beckett, and

James Joyce. The first time I experienced this phenomenon was when I was consulting about writing in a middle school in the South Bronx. A teacher who attended my workshop at her school came up to me during a break and said, "I have a young man in my eighth-grade class, and I don't know what to do with his writing. It's bizarre! Please, could you take a look at it and tell me what I could do with him?" This poor teacher looked genuinely overwhelmed by Tyrell's particular issues. She knew there was something wonderful about it, but it did not meet any of the standard criteria of conventional, school-sanctioned writing. I took Tyrell's notebook to read during my lunch break. I cannot recall what labels or classifications he had received, but my memory is that he had been held back a year. His writing astonished me, and I asked if I could meet him and perhaps work with him during my lunch breaks whenever I worked at this school.

I had never seen writing like this from a young person. In the pages of a spiral notebook, in flowing handwriting, spilled page after page of the most complicated, inventive, confused, and often frightfully beautiful prose I had ever seen. In all honesty, if I had not been Lucy Calkins' student and had not read her brilliant first book, *Lessons from a Child*, I may not have known where to begin, beyond circling obvious spelling and punctuation errors. But I remembered how carefully and respectfully she had made a case study of one young girl's writing process; how she had taken on the role of researcher, looking for a "window onto a child's thinking" instead of feeling "exasperated by error" (1983, 56). I wanted to become a researcher, and look upon Tyrell as a fascinating case study, and know that, as Calkins writes, "When we regard our students as unique and fascinating, when they become case-study subjects even while they are students, then the children become our teachers, showing us how they learn" (8). So in order to notice and name the beauty and brilliance in Tyrell's work, I had to reach into my knowledge of what contemporary writers do with language and text forms and compare that with what I saw in this young man's writing.

Tyrell made up all kinds of fancy words, such as *accentment* and *ordinarial*. They seemed overreaching in some way, perhaps toward a "Standard English"; as June Jordan says, his words were "stilted, and frequently polysyllabic, simply for the sake of having more syllables" (2002, 161). On several pages, he wrote only two sentences that still impress me with their slanted beauty: "Daybreak is on its curve. The birds glisten and the branches wobble." As a poet, I would have to revise ten times to get lines so original and mellifluous. First of all, *daybreak*: what fifteen-year-old boy says "daybreak"? *On its curve*: as if the light bends and echoes the shape of the world. *Birds glisten*: Tyrell flips our expectations for what birds do (chirp, sing, caw?) and draws our attention to a visual aspect, as if morning dew shone on their feathers. *Branches wobble*: again, an idea that surprises. We might think of leaves rustling in the wind or branches swaying in the wind. Here, we don't know if there's wind or not, and I've never heard of a branch "wobbling" before.

What happens after these opening sentences changes on every page; sometimes a full page of what seems to be fictional prose follows, sometimes just a paragraph. If I were to guess at his writing process, I would say it's as if he knows that opening sentence, "Daybreak is on its curve" is a keeper, but he has to keep jump-starting the story because he's never satisfied. In various versions, we are inside a cathedral at a "wedding of somewhat incandescent value." There is variously a priest or a Father, whose life is either "a burning ship in no mercy" or "a knot you couldn't quite untangle." The overall tone of every page, though there are some funny and odd details, is dark and depressed; not much happens, but a lot of dense, intriguing description about subjects that seemed way too mature for a fifteen-year-old boy, if you ask me.

Finally, when I was able to meet with Tyrell, this is what I said: "You are an exquisite writer! You remind me of my favorite writers, Gwendolyn Brooks, James Joyce, Jeanette Winterson, and Samuel Beckett, all at once!" And then I asked him what I was dying to know: "What do you read?"

"The Bible," Tyrell said.

Of course! The church setting, the dense, old-fashioned prose, and even the kind of dark overtones reminded me of my own experiences with liturgy as a child. I was able to meet with Tyrell only two times. I brought my copy of James Joyce's *Ulysses* with me and showed him the first page that begins:

Stately, plump Buck Mulligan came down from the stairhead, bearing a bowl of lather on which a mirror and a razor lay crossed. A yellow dressinggown, ungirdled, was sustained gently behind him by the mild morning air. He held the bowl aloft and intoned:
    —*Introibo ad altare Dei.*

We shouldn't compare kids writing only to famous (or dead) writers, though. We can show kids that their writing is similar to contemporary short fiction, graphic novels, digital interactive texts, and other texts that defy all genre rules. When I conferred with Tyrell, there was no Internet, so besides *Ulysses*, I also showed him some pages from an unusual and gorgeous memoir that I was reading at the time. *Under the Eye of the Clock,* narrated in third person by Irish poet, Christopher Nolan, is about growing up with severe cerebral palsy; its radically musical prose won awards and had critics comparing him with James Joyce and Dylan Thomas.

> Christened for his cross-bearing, he chalk-white weathered the avenues of his babyhood. But nobody wounded like him could deserve a chance at life. Better dead said the crones, better dead said history, better jump in at the deep end decided her strong soul as she heard his crestfallen cry. His mother it was who treated him as normal, tumbled to his intelligence, tumbled to his eye-signalled talk, tumbled to the hollyberries, green yet, but holding promise of burning in red given time, given home. (1987, 50)

Joyce, Nolan, Brooks, and Virginia Woolf, these are the writers I suggested Tyrell try reading—why not, his writing sounded just like theirs—along with his Bible, in hopes that he could find himself among the greats. Every time I look at the copy I kept, these many years later, I think Tyrell's writing is still the most lyrical and inventive I have ever seen from a young person.

What If We Build a Writing Curriculum from Strength?

My hope is that as teachers we respond to all students' writing with astonished, appreciative, awestruck eyes. But we can't create this kind of writing response if we don't first "fall in love" with our students' quirky, unconventional, and culture-infused texts. Writing teacher-extraordinaire, Brenda Ueland, wrote back in 1938 that "The only good teachers . . . are those who love you, who think you are interesting or very important, or wonderfully funny; whose attitude is: 'Tell me more. Tell me all you can. I want to understand more about everything you feel and know and all the changes inside and out of you'" (1987, 8). So what if we were to gather our courage and read student writing wanting to know more? With the belief that our student writers are interesting and "wonderfully funny"? With eyes to see the beauty and brilliance in our students' writing rather than the lack of topic sentences at the beginning of each paragraph?

What if we were to suspend the mandates, real or simply perceived, from our administrations, districts, state, and federal governments, to read deeply, and reread, and attempt to understand what our students are writing?

What if we were able to read and respond to work by children who write so gorgeously and ingeniously that we are at a loss of what to suggest they try to do to improve? And what if we were able to champion even the most spindly pieces of writing by digging in and envisioning what is there, assigning the same generous amounts of time and respect we give to the most difficult of published literature?

Since writing reflects thoughts and feelings, and bares the self more than any other activity that children will undertake in school, it also tends to reflect the differences between children. What if we help create spaces for each and every child behind the writing—kids who have difficulty in school, kids who are quirky and outrageous, kids who don't fit in the boxes that standards, rubrics, and tests have forced us to draw—to shine?

What This Book Will Do

This book will teach you how to notice, perhaps even love, the hidden beauty in student writing that will help you feel excited by what your students know and can do.

In this book, I suggest ways to build a writing curriculum from strength, rather than from what is missing or what mistakes immediately leap from our students' drafts. Like most adults, when I read kids' writing, I too am almost swallowed up in a sea of punctuation errors, twisted syntax, shifting tenses, and underdeveloped ideas. I have to take a step back and ask myself where this radar for error came from so that I can question and critique it. Then I have to fill my store of alternatives for reading kids' writing. Because when I'm able to read past all those surface problems, what I find in young people's writing is passionate, surprising, and endearing enough to convince me that I have the best job on the earth.

Part 1 of the book invites readers to think along with me about how we have made our knowledge of what we see and say about student writing—our lenses for reading their work. Once we know what our lenses are and where they came from, we can decide which ones are useful for our students, and which might need tweaking or even discarding. We can also think about adding to the possibilities for response through our own reading and writing, and by inventing fun new ways to talk about the qualities of good writing. With dozens of options for naming what we see, we explore how to respond to student writing, whether in writing conferences, share sessions, in the margins of drafts, in family/student conferences, in blogs or tweets.

In particular, I slow down the writing conference, the one-to-one instructional conversation between teacher and student during a writing workshop. Calkins (1994) described the parts of a writing conference as Research, Decide, and Teach. I want to add a second step—Name—where we listen and look for something a student is doing that we can build from and reinforce, to offer a "lasting compliment," as Calkins, Hartman, and White call it (2005, 64). We name something specific, something that writers honestly do or at least try to do, that we can see or hear in a student's piece already. I believe this *naming* portion of the writing conference is not a throwaway moment, not empty praise, or a pat on the head for being a good girl or boy, but in fact the key to *teaching* students something they may not have consciously realized they are doing so that they can build on it and do it again. I find that kids learn more from this naming of their capabilities and that the information goes deeper and stays longer than even my most enlightened minilesson or teaching point in a conference does. When writing feels hard, and believe me, it does for everyone, what pulls you through, what helps you solve all the little knots and puzzle places, and makes you "sit and stay" (as Katie Wood Ray calls the reality of a writer's work) is not knowing what "nominative absolute" means but knowing what your particular writing passions, talents, and quirks are. You don't get true, fire-in-the-belly energy for writing because you fear getting a bad grade but because you have something to say and your own way of saying it.

In this book, I hope to expand a thinking and feeling for diversity in writing, so that we can find and name the particular voice that students send out to the world every time they put pen to paper or fingers to keyboard, rather than narrow the possibilities for writing that most evaluation and grading does. I hope to move toward a culturally accepting practice, a liberal kind of growth, rather than the anemic categories that most school-sanctioned assessment practices would allow.

In Part 2 of the book, I read pieces of student writing through the lens of someone who writes as often as possible and reads a variety of texts. Novelist Toni Morrison (2006, 174) says that there is a difference between reading as a skill and reading as an *art*. To read like an artist, she says, involves "digging for the hidden, questioning or relishing the choices the author made, . . . eager to envision what is there." I like to apply this idea to reading student writing. I like to try to imagine that in the scrawniest, most illegible piece of writing, I will be able to find what that student was meaning to say, though it may be hidden from me at first.

Chapters 6 and 7 invite readers to honor student writing the way we would honor a novel by Toni Morrison, Jonathan Safran Foer, or Barbara Kingsolver. Travel with me as I dig into and envision pieces written by young, unseasoned writers, the way we would inquire our way into a poem by Nikki Giovanni, Julia Alvarez, Jimmy Santiago Baca, or Naomi Shihab Nye, and try to read it like an artist, as Toni Morrison says. Perhaps this way of reading can renew our *faith*, as Donald Murray names it, that all of our students "have something to say and a language in which to say it" (1982, 160). "I hear voices from my students they have never heard from themselves. I find they are authorities on subjects they think ordinary. Sometimes I lose that faith," Murray writes, "but if I regain it and do not interfere, my students do write and I begin to hear things that need saying said well" (160). After I name several positive aspects of each piece of writing, I offer two or three directions for what I might teach the writer how to do next in writing if he or she were my student.

In Chapter 8, I present practical ideas for reading student work with colleagues in order to help each other expand the horizons for what to see and say about students' writing. I offer specific guidelines and protocols for how to read the writing, along with grids or templates for storing what everyone finds so that you can take the comments immediately back to your students. In the final chapters, I explore options to writing response through positive assessment and through the ultimate in response: writing celebrations.

What This Book Will Teach

This book will teach you new ways to name what you see in student writing so that it motivates kids to want to write more and revise for readers.

Some student writing, especially in middle and high school, gets labeled "below grade level" or scored with a 1 on a four-point scale because its syntax differs from conventional English or it struggles with a shape or logical order that helps readers uncover the meaning. Also, much student writing concerns topics we may dislike or prefer not to read about, like replays of cartoons and video games, blow-by-blow descriptions of soccer games, and graphic stories of desperate home lives that are beyond our imaginations. So when we confer with these writers or remark with our pens in the margins of their papers, we might have to work to find specific, positive things to say. But find them, we must. "In so many ways we are creations of language, the things that people have said to us, the things they tell us we are," says poet Linda Hogan (2001, 121), whose memoir, *The Woman Who Watches Over the World*, explores pain and healing inside her personal and Native American tribal history. I agree with Hogan that the language we use with our students has the power to create who they become as writers. I know that telling a young person that her writing voice slides around your shoulders and warms you is language that might create her as a writer and a person eager to learn more. Continually naming the same child as "low-performing" on state writing tests is language that might construct her as a failure for the rest of her life.

Sometimes I notice when I speak appreciatively of student writing, people have a look on their face that seems to say, "Where is she coming up with this stuff?" I think I learned ways of talking about student writing from reading and taking writing classes in which I learned from others how to talk about writing. I learned it, too, because I often have to work to see the value in my own writing. While these experiences help me know how to make visible what often seems, at first glance, invisible, I know that all teachers can learn to read like writers, to have more informed lenses, and to expand their vocabulary for talking about writing. This book will help provide that new language.

My purpose in this book is to demonstrate that student writers often perform remarkable feats in the craft of writing, from the macro level of content and organization, to the micro level of sentences, images, and word choice, precisely *because* they are young, unpracticed writers. They haven't yet conformed to notions of conventional syntax or fixed and formulaic genre structures, so their writing sounds fresh and original, ahead of its time, avant-garde you could even say. Pablo Picasso apparently said that every child is an artist. He also claimed that it took him four years to paint like Raphael, but a lifetime to paint like a child. As a writer of poetry and nonfiction, I understand that desire for the unbridled imagination of a child. I also admire, almost envy, the inventive ways that children use language. I believe that if we acquire content knowledge about how to read and talk about writing, we can begin to appreciate the gifts of childlike expression. Using the discourse of artists rather than the more abstract and often damaging evaluations fostered by tests, letter grades, and hyperattention to surface conventions, we will be able to notice and name the specific technique each student is using. Students with writing difficulties feel better about writing and want to keep doing it when they have a sense of what they do particularly well. Strong writers more readily take risks with their writing by trying new styles, new genres, and new sophisticated techniques when they have some names for their attempts and accomplishments. All of our students will have a place in this community of writers we build in our classrooms—a community that will rise from the earth and face all its sources of inspiration.

What Voices Dance in Our Heads as We Read Student Writing, and Where Did They Come From?

I believe it is important to review our own histories as young writers receiving comments and grades on our nascent drafts. So I'll begin this chapter with a little exercise for you to try on your own or with colleagues. Here are the steps of this exercise:

1. In your own middle school, high school, or college experience, what are some comments about your writing from family members, teachers, or professors that linger in your memory as being especially helpful or hurtful? Which comments felt like a warm hug or stung you and perhaps haunt you still? Comments may have come from casual assessments or formal grades, test scores, or evaluations. They may have been spoken or written. I trust that there is a reason the comments remain memorable, and so I invite you to take a full ten minutes to complete this list. You might make a double-column entry in your notebook (as shown below), or you might invent your own kind of graphic organizer to answer the questions. You might also try a quick timeline to help you focus your memory.

Helped or "hugged"	Hurt or "stung"

2. Look back over the comments and note beside them any surprises. Notice patterns and themes. Do the comments often refer to the same kind of writing feature: organization, sentence structure, comma use, word choice, or content development? Note the conditions of the writing task itself: Did the writing happen at home or at school? Was the writing piece assigned or self-initiated?

3. Write and reflect for a few minutes about how the experiences on your list could have shaped the writer (or nonwriter) you are today.

4. Now, talk with a colleague or friend for another ten minutes about what you noticed. What commonalities arise in your experiences with writing response? Did either of you receive a response that made a difference in your lifelong feeling for writing, either positively or negatively? What was the nature of that standout response? What generalizations can you make about response to writing as you look at your timelines? What type of response—written or verbal—helped you feel powerful as a writer, and what kind of comments discouraged you?

Colleagues from the Teachers College Reading and Writing Project and I have introduced some variant of this exercise for almost three decades when we invite teachers to work on their own writing in summer institute sections. We have been intrigued to find that teachers' answers remain constant, no matter their age or experience. If we had been collecting teachers' timelines, two-column graphic organizers, and notebook reflections on those items, we would by now have a computer full of data supporting two truth claims: negative comments on writing result in lifelong anxiety about and avoidance of writing; positive comments result in lifelong ease and confidence in writing. "Language can deeply wound, and leave lasting scars," Ralph Fletcher writes. "On the other hand, the words we speak can be crucial missing ingredients to help a kid make a breakthrough in his writing" (2006, 109).

If you're like most teachers we've worked with on this exercise, you might have received some As that gave you a flush of self-worth. You might have had a poem published in high school, or an essay read aloud as a sample of what the teacher considered exemplary writing. One teacher, Traci Jackson, a teacher in White Plains, New York, wrote a paper in college that was turned back with this inscription at the top: "Your writing is simple, yet elegant." Traci said she has lived her life with those words guiding not only her writing, but also her way of being in the world. Her teacher truly nailed it, or perhaps Traci grew into those words, once she had been named with them because this gorgeous woman exudes elegance in her voice, mannerisms, and gracious style. Other teachers in my course that summer loved Traci's story, and we kept joyfully weaving the phrase "simple, yet elegant" into all our conversations for the rest of the week.

From your comments list, you may notice that you received lots of big red As on your papers, but you didn't know precisely *what* about your writing made it worthy of an A. As a college student, I received mostly positive comments on my writing content and composition, but the one time I made a B on a literary analysis essay, it practically made me quit school! My contemporary literature professor (my favorite teacher, no less; this was my fourth class with him) wrote next to that B: "This smacks of creative writing." Ouch! Those words burn me to this day. I happened to be taking several creative writing classes at the time, so I believed he must have been right to recognize their influences, but why was that a *bad* thing? There were no other comments on the entire twelve-page paper, so I never understood what I had done to fall from his good graces. Back in those days, no one questioned their grades, so I didn't have the guts to ask him to explain either.

Most of us remember papers with misspelled words circled in red and comments in the margins, such as *vague*, *wordy*, and *awkward* (or sometimes just the diminutive, *AWK*). Don't you wonder if that word *awkward* was in some teachers guide of how to respond to student writing? What aspect of our writing did *awkward* refer to? What was *AWK* about it? I certainly recognize and relate to the mind-numbing, tailbone-bruising consequences of grading hundreds and hundreds of papers, perhaps spurring high school and college composition teachers to shorten *awkward* to *AWK*. (I heard there might even be premade rubber stamps with those words on them!) I've decided that the word itself represents an unease in teachers' minds, when they are not sure *why*, grammatically speaking, a sentence doesn't work, but it just doesn't sound or look right. Again, I can relate.

Unfortunately, students learning to write do not learn anything about how to revise from a scribbled *AWK* in the margin. To a young person, his sentence says what he wants it to say. Literate—that is, *written* versus *oral*—grammar structures are learned from reading a great deal of written texts. Kids have perhaps not been given enough time to read or have not been invited to study how sentences are built inside the stories, articles, and novels they are reading, so their early attempts at sentence structure mimic the fragmented, disjointed ways of talking and thinking natural to all humans, from politicians, to physics and English professors, to our family members.

Look over your memory list again, and try to grasp what productive or destructive comments look, sound, and especially, feel like. Teachers have told me moving stories of feeling noticed, truly "seen" for their specific writing gifts. Sarah Hopkins, a teacher at Ward Elementary in Clear Creek, Texas, remembered a college professor suggesting that she should try to get one of her papers published in a journal or education magazine. When Sarah said those words out loud to the group, she blushed with pride. Much more often, though, teachers tell stories of feeling cut down, almost brutalized by verbal and written comments on their work. Maggie Bills, a teacher from Townshend, Vermont, remembers all too vividly that her kindergarten teacher would not hang her work on the wall with everyone else's because she had accidentally added an extra *g* to her own name: "Magggie." Her teacher made a big red X through the third *g* and gave it back to her. Imagine that little five-year-old girl, who learned in the space of perhaps thirty seconds that one pencil mark on a piece of paper could cause this adult whom she wanted desperately to please to react with such anger and disgust. Maggie is an example of someone who became a lifelong learner and caring teacher *despite* that horrid experience.

Janet Fitch, author of the best-selling novels, *White Oleander, Paint It Black,* and *Kicks,* a young adult novel, tells about writing her first short story when she was nine years old. "I combined my favorite authors: Marguerite Henry, who wrote horse stories, and Edgar Allan Poe. My story was called 'Diamond: Horse of Mystery'. . . . I was in a public school, in a class of 40 students. I thought I could get the teacher's attention by showing her the story, but all she did was take a red pen and mark all over it, correcting the spelling, grammar, and punctuation. She didn't say a thing about the story itself. I didn't write again until I was 21" (2006, 278). Stories abound of famous writers who received comments from teachers such as "You will never be a writer" or "You have a B mind," and have never quite recovered from that. Writers are rare who pursued their craft despite, or perhaps because of, the critical comments. Most adults would rather dig a ditch beside a highway in the August sun than write something. When I work with a group of teachers, someone will point out that despite sob stories of tactless writing response from childhood, we all became teachers anyway. True enough. But I counter that we represent a tiny slice of the population. For dozens of reasons, we have risen above our bad memories, perhaps wishing to become better teachers than some we experienced ourselves. Janet Fitch is an example of someone who persevered as a writer because she had to; she is a storyteller. But I would lay bets that her teacher's red marks continue to haunt her, even after she has successfully published three novels. I have met literally hundreds of adults who remain so scarred from inconsiderate, harsh comments that they fear and avoid writing except when forced to produce. As we write, the "Proofreading Parrot," as I call it, sits on our shoulders, trained to see and say the same things over and over and never shuts up: "comma splice!" "fragment!" "squawk!" A teacher in one of my workshops said that all she was concerned about while writing in school was "trying to get less and less red ink." Does any of this sound familiar or describe you? What is your story?

Our responses to young people learning to write matter more than we can ever know. Yet often, we are at a loss for exactly *what* to say when faced with an illegible jumble of words, or a spindly paragraph where there should be many pages of text. How can we spin something positive to say when inside we're just feeling frustrated at how much we still need to teach? At the other end of the spectrum, we might also feel stumped when we read work by kids, who at nine, twelve, or sixteen, can write circles around us. Sometimes we can only say, "That's great! Keep going!" and scurry on.

One way to help us find words to say about our students' writing is to remember those comments that felt meaningful and supportive when we were students. Or we can listen to and borrow from the positive comments that have burned like eternal flames inside our friends' and colleagues' hearts all these years. In my senior year of high school, Paula (Eyrich) Tyler, my creative writing teacher, set the course for the rest of my life when she simply said, "You are a poet and you have a poet's soul." I've definitely used that one with plenty of kids. Over a decade later, when novelist and memoirist, Geoffrey Wolfe read early drafts of my memoir, his bold black permanent-penned comments in the margins were only positive and encouraging.

But it was what Wolfe said to me in a writing conference that remains stamped upon my brain, that keeps me believing I can and should write, in those dark nights of the soul when I'm feeling most unsure of myself. In one chapter of my memoir, I had tried to re-create a typical scene around my childhood dinner table. I telescoped hundreds of such evenings into one scene, explaining that this is how it usually went. Wolfe said my description of the dinner table routine in my childhood was so vivid, so delicately painted and so restrained of any blame or anger that he thought he could hear and see the little girl that was me. He said that he wanted to reach into the words and hold that little girl.

This comment gave me a name for what I was doing, mostly unconsciously at that time, in my writing. Then it became my personal standard for good writing—restraint. It became a high-quality bar that I try to hurdle whenever I write. Now, as a teacher of writing, I sometimes recycle this comment almost verbatim! It comes out of my mouth during conferences or from my pen while reading student writing, when I imagine myself inside a sad or angry moment a student describes plainly and simply.

I think what Wolfe did, actually, was to read my writing as if he were reading a published memoir, even though I was just a student in his class. Wolfe found a place in my writing that he could talk about as if he were a member of a book club discussing the latest book selection. He elevated my work, and therefore elevated my identity: I became "one who writes and moves readers" just as he does, just as all the authors on our favorite books list and bookshelves do.

The particular words we use with our students to comment on their writing have tremendous power and weight, as Peter Johnston (2004) argues in his hugely important book, beloved by many, called *Choice Words*: "Speaking is as much an action as hitting someone with a stick, or hugging them" (8). Words hurt and words help. Often, saying something makes it so. A jury can send someone to life in prison or set someone free just with the words *guilty* or *not guilty*. Johnston notes that "Language then, is not merely *representational* (though it is that); it is also *constitutive*. It actually creates realities and invites identities" (9). Teachers can help create kids who love to write and try to improve their writing by naming their hidden gems, their particular gifts as writers. Or we can destroy any desire to write by constantly pointing out what is wrong or what is missing. We can be what Robert Probst calls a "hunter of errors" (1989, 74) and Alan Purves calls a "copy editor/proof reader" (74). As these two researchers point out, students who figure out that spelling, punctuation, and grammar are merely puzzles, games to play to win the prize of an A, begin to write to please those "copy editors," rather than write for meaning or to discover their own writing identity and process.

Kids begin to grow their identities as writers from the first mark they place on a page. We hope they receive lots of enthusiasm and encouragement from family members for their treasure maps, get-well cards, recipes for making colored ice, diagrams for robot parts, and princess stories. But when they enter school, the picture turns bleak for what writing is supposed to look like, circumscribed by assessments, evaluations, letter grades, and rubric scores. School becomes the place to be wrong and writing becomes a place to find or "ferret out," as Daiker (1989, 104) puts it, surface and structural errors. A text's emotion, meaning, and intention take a back seat to so-called correctness. The research of Daly and Miller shows that students who have received mostly critical attention for the errors in their papers become anxious and "high apprehensive writers" (Daiker 1989, 105). They avoid any kind of writing; they find college majors and jobs that require the least amount of writing. When they must write, they choose "less intense" language than more comfortable writers. High apprehensive writers use "fewer words and make fewer statements" (106). The more they avoid writing, of course, the less they learn how to write, and without the continual practice it takes to improve, these students solidify their identities as writers who get low grades and negative comments on their papers—failure heaped upon failure. As Anthony Inzerillo, principal at PS 199 in Queens, says, "It's like teaching my daughter Melanie to catch a ball, and it goes *boomp* in her face. If I say, 'Great, Melanie! You put your arms out!' she'll want to try it again. Or I could say, 'Geez! Melanie! You really can't catch a ball can you?' She'll just quit trying."

I cringe to think that young people whose writing has been scrutinized and given the red-pen equivalent of "Geez! You really can't write can you?" might just quit trying, and might determine their life interests, or retreat from meaningful life's work, based on how much writing will be involved. It saddens me that any adult would not use writing as a tool for solving work or life problems or for journaling their way through anger or grief. One problem with a large focus on surface features in writing is that young people don't yet have a system for when and where to place a comma when they have had relatively little opportunity to write or to develop a system for caring about writing in the first place. Constant attention to and judgment on mechanics and organization becomes a systematic means for placing restraints on kids without listening to what they have to say.

> Young people . . . might determine their life's work . . . based on how much writing will be involved.

Research about writing response claims that praise and encouragement take writing a greater distance than criticism. "Paul B. Diederich, senior research associate for the Educational Testing Service, concluded from his research in evaluation that 'noticing and praising whatever a student does well improves writing more than any kind or amount of correction of what he does badly, and that it is especially important for the less able writers who need all the encouragement they can get'" (Daiker 1989, 105). Apparently then, according to Diederich's research, even just saying "That's great; keep going!" teaches more than circling errors.

Several education theorists, psychologists, and researchers, perhaps most famously Carol S. Dweck, Alfie Kohn, and Peter Johnston, caution against using empty praise, rewards, or grades for teaching young people. In her popular books and articles, Dweck cites research with thousands of children from age four to adolescence that showed that praise, especially saying that a child is "smart," produces a "short burst of pride, followed by a long string of negative consequences" (2007, 36). When children were told at home or in school that they were "smart," it created in the kids a "fixed mind-set," where they believed they have a predetermined, innate (and limited) amount of intelligence and cannot learn. If parents and teachers focused instead on kids' learning process, how they solve a problem, how they practice, look things up, and ask for help, the children developed a "growth mind-set," and believed they could always improve with effort. Dweck writes, "Effort or 'process' praise (praise for engagement, perseverance, strategies, improvement, and the like) fosters hardy motivation. It tells students what they've done to be successful and what they need to do to be successful again in the future" (36).

If you had followed me day by day in my writing classroom, listened in to my writing conferences, and read the response notes I wrote on five-inch-by-seven-inch sticky notes to my kids, you would have seen mostly Dweck's "process praise," comments about the strategies kids used in their writing as well as evidence of trying new strategies and improving on areas we had pinpointed together to grow. (And yes, there were definitely some phrases like "You're doing it! Keep going!" thrown in to our incredibly active, humming, workshop environment.) But in every writing conference, especially at the beginning of the year, you would have heard me naming what my kids knew and could do as writers, in language that other writers and artists use to talk about their craft. You would have heard many of the examples and suggestions that are in this book, especially in Chapters 3 and 4. I agree with Dweck that calling someone "smart" can actually terrify and freeze a young person; what do they do if they don't understand something or if they get a wrong answer? They're supposed to be so "smart"! And "smartness" definitely does not translate to strong writing; in fact, when I confer with kids who have been given labels like "gifted and talented," they often reject the idea of revising their drafts or refuse to write in front of me because they are afraid of making mistakes or not knowing something. Instead, we can all learn how to name precise writing qualities in our students' work once we push past our deeply ingrained notions of what makes writing "good" and "bad."

Where Did We Learn What Writing Should Look and Sound Like?

When we read a piece of student writing, try as we might, we are probably unable to read with any neutrality or lack of personal bias. Writing teachers approach student writing with particular lenses—I call them the "voices that dance in our heads"—that inform our reading and responding. "What a teacher says to a student about writing is saturated with the teacher's values, beliefs, and models of learning," Chris Anson points out (1989, 354). These "saturated" beliefs and methods of responding were given to us throughout our own education and life experiences. Let's look at some of the origins of our approaches to reading and assessing student writing and try to figure out what might be considered reasonable foundations for writing instruction and what might now feel inadequate or inaccurate, given tremendous upheavals in the last thirty years in the field of writing theory and composition.

Our High School English and College Composition Classes

When I published my first book for teachers, I learned how many of the rules I had so carefully memorized and shown off in my English classes were no longer considered correct, and my manuscripts came back to me covered in red ink again, but this time for *following* the rules I'd learned in school!

The good news is: teaching sticks. When our teachers told us the same thing year in and year out—indent your paragraphs five spaces; *i* before *e* except after *c*—we generally took that to heart and we probably repeat it to ourselves as we write, even today. If we had a terrific writing teacher who knew about composing and revising, genre forms, and reading/writing connections, we likely have a strong sense of what to look for in a piece of student writing.

The bad news is that teaching sticks! We all know what to teach largely from what we have been taught. If we had teachers (more than one, certainly) who harped on handwriting, spelling, punctuation, and paragraphing, then those are the things that instantly leap off the page when we read our students' writing. Certain kinds of errors (such as "me and my friend went . . .") can actually cause frenzy amongst language arts teachers. Wall and Hull (1989) note that grammar guides and handbooks frequently label "very commonplace usages of *OK* and *hopefully* and *irregardless* as examples of language use that are *detestable* and *vulgar* and *idiotic* and *oafish*" (261). As I've mentioned, many of our ideas of correctness are "value-laden" at best and incorrect, at worst.

Some rules that we memorized in middle school and high school no longer apply to written texts yet continue to haunt our heads and our red pens. Ed Schuster (2003), author of my favorite rabble-rousing grammar book, *breaking the rules* (yes, his title even breaks the rules; it's not capitalized!), calls these ghosts of high school English "mythrules" and proceeds to divulge the history and origin of each and also gives dozens of examples of broken rules in all our favorite authors, including Shakespeare. It is perfectly fine, for instance, to end a sentence with a preposition; not doing so can result in convoluted sentences that sound terrible when you read them out loud. Another extinct rule: sentences should *never* begin with a conjunction. This is incorrect, and in fact, a reader can examine thousands of published texts to see this supposed rule broken again and again. A more reasonable approach to the frequent overuse of *and* at the beginning of sentences is first to recognize that this practice mimics oral language and storytelling, which uses *and* to connect sentences and parts so that the listener can easily follow the sequence and logic. Next, we might demonstrate with written text, how many of those sentences can be combined, dropping the *and* to create stronger, more succinct sentences. Rather than beginning with the mistakes students make, we could start by realizing that students are *transitioning* from the way that people speak to a more formal literate style.

Well-Meaning Family Members and Friends

Our parents and relatives wanted the best for us so often they made sure we did well in school, and they made sure we got the best grades on spelling, handwriting, and grammar worksheets. These were the kind of worksheets our parents remember doing when they were in school, and they either suffered over it and got low grades, in which case they yearn for things to go better for us, or they were quite skilled at the skills, in which case we had better be the same or even better at it than they were.

Parents may have corrected our spoken errors in an unduly harsh manner: "It's *ran*, not *runned!*" They may have marked up our homework or letters to relatives, circling the misspellings or adding in commas. Siblings and cousins may have edited our speech and writing because this is one way we learned early on that it's possible to ridicule and demonstrate power over someone in ways that aren't physical and punishable.

Notions of correctness in grammar and spelling may have become, for many of us, places of personal failure in the eyes of those closest to us. As adults, and as teachers, we may bring those lessons unwittingly to our students as we read and comment on their writing.

District Mandates, Standards, Curriculum Frameworks

When I bring literacy professional development to schools, I often counsel teachers and principals to collaborate toward a vision of what they want quality writing instruction, process, and product to look like in their particular school (see Chapter 8). But if that vision builds solely or primarily on skills acquisition—*all seventh graders must demonstrate knowledge of sentence diagramming*—then the resulting curriculum framework can feel reductive, restrictive, and evaluative. We aim to follow the lead of our school and our colleagues for helping our students achieve, yet we end up narrowing the lenses we look through as we assess our students' writing. Those students who can fulfill the restrictive list of skills and concepts get the prize, and the rest struggle or fail, creating a community of haves and have nots.

When I taught fifth grade, my colleagues and I were handed a list of expected skills and concepts to be covered throughout the year in writing. Here is a tiny taste—

only ten out of twenty-four items—of the joyful writing curriculum that awaited my students and me each year:

- spelling
- handwriting
- capitalization
- conjunctions
- parts of speech
- prepositional phrases
- contractions
- root words
- dialogue
- suspense

Only the last two items could arguably be about composing written texts rather than isolated grammar or mechanics skills. The list is grossly generalized, not specific at all, and it has no compass or guide for how to teach these isolated items. Still, the list hung like an axe over the head of my teaching team, causing us to read our students' writing in a kind of panic, searching for evidence of mastery over these skills and concepts, and wailing in anguish because we could not find it.

Let's face it; teachers are generally a rule-following lot. We don't like to make waves; we were the "good students" in our own childhood classrooms, and we got lots of rewards for being good. So when we're told by school administrations, state education officials, and now by federal officials in the Department of Education what and how to teach, we tend to obey. The problem is that often those officials are wrong. If what they tell us to do ignores the particular, individual children in our classrooms, then I believe that is wrong. If they dictate how we should teach without knowing who *teachers* are, if they fail to consider our ability to think and make decisions based on the living processes of our classrooms, then I believe they are wrong.

Published Writing Programs and Rubrics

By *published writing programs and rubrics*, I mean the type produced by large publishing companies that researched state standards and writing test rubrics and formed lessons, worksheets, and evaluative rubrics to match those standards. It all makes sense, doesn't it? If you are required to teach this list, and then your district can purchase a program that provides blackline master worksheets and tells you how to teach that list and how to grade it, who wouldn't want that? The problem is that most of these programs ignore the specific children and teachers in specific classrooms and most deliver isolated skills practice and do not make room for what is a messy, recursive process and a way of thinking on the page and communicating with readers.

Now, for several reasons, you gotta love a good rubric. I remember that when I had to grade hundreds of college freshman essays, I saved myself time, energy, and dozens of student questions and complaints by making a type of rubric and giving it to my students before they wrote. This enabled them to write to my prescribed expectations, and then I could simply put checkmarks in the boxes according to whether they fulfilled the requirements. If anyone wanted to argue a grade, I could just point to the rubric and say, "Here's what you were supposed to do, and here's how you didn't do it."

Yuck! I hate seeing those words flowing from my fingertips. This is what the system of grading and ranking creates—a reliance on external criteria and a kind of blindness to any stray brilliance or beauty that wanders outside the boxes. Writing is not flour or water or fat; it cannot be objectively measured. Writing is not a set of morals or laws; it cannot be judged good or bad. So while rubrics offer a vast improvement over empty letter or number grades in that they provide descriptors of expectations for writing, they are still not fast enough or huge enough to catch the winds of writing. Maja Wilson, in her brilliant book *Rethinking Rubrics*, lays out the best argument against them and in the most beautiful and engaging prose of any book about assessment I've read. She argues that rubrics claim certain linear factors of writing that can be weighed and measured reliably enough for teachers to be able to judge good and bad writing. "However, writing may not be a simple system like billiards, subject to the laws of determinism. Writing may more closely resemble complex, chaotic systems like global weather, economic systems, or political unrest" (2006, 32).

Rubrics also largely rely on what Tom Newkirk calls a "formalist tradition," for evaluating writing that "presume[s] to isolate 'qualities' of good writing as if they existed irrespective of content and blind to the cultural and ideological biases that inevitably come into play" (1997, 6). For example, while rubrics frequently evaluate *voice* in student writing, what counts as quality *voice* in the minds of the readers and scorers of countless student essays often includes three- and four-syllable words ("sparkle words," and "juicy words" as I've heard them described to kids), a rash of similes, and multiple awkward substitutions for the word *said*, while a writer's true voice might contain slang, code-switching from one language to another, and dialect, all of which might return marked as incorrect.

And finally, rubrics cannot begin to describe the complex joys and sorrows of a piece of writing, and yet as they are used in school systems, they do define young people's writing identities. That is why I do not care for rubrics or grading of writing of any kind, especially with young writers who are just beginning to shape their writing identities. I guarantee that most kids who come to know themselves as C writers, or number 2 writers, or whatever the hierarchical classification system exists, remain a C or a 2 in their minds and hearts and become adults who hate to write.

Grades

As with rubric evaluation, grades on poems, stories, articles, and essays cannot possibly be objective. There is nothing to count and measure in writing except the number of paragraphs, T-units (sentences), and errors. "Grading, even in a portfolio, freezes student work and teacher commentary," writes Brian Huot (2002, 73), my most trusted expert on writing assessment. Grades stop thinking because kids either become focused on what a particular teacher expects or defines as necessary to get an A or students become fearful of judgment, of being wrong. Grades define writing identities—I am a C writer—in vague, subjective, and indeterminate ways that do not help kids learn how to take responsibility for revising and editing or develop their writing voices.

For a larger discussion of how to deal with the fact that most of us are required as part of our jobs to assign writing grades to older students, see Chapter 9. For now, I simply list grading as another aspect of an external system that puts pressure on how we approach response to student writing. Grades not only suppress student learning, they suppress teaching as an act of inquiry and exploration with students. Grades position teachers as arbiters of excellence and failure, and do not allow us to act intelligently inside our profession.

Our Own Preferences, Expectations, and Comfort Levels

Jimmy Williams, a compassionate, intelligent teacher in Austin, Texas, admitted, in front of over one hundred people at a workshop I led, that in the past, he had read student writing through the lenses of his own moods and prejudices. His honesty moved the rest of us to recognize this truth in ourselves. We are human, and some days we simply can't find it in ourselves to even read, much less wax poetic about yet another illegible or incomprehensible piece of writing. Jimmy admits that he has evolved as a teacher, and that is what we all aim for, through continuous reading of professional books, attending workshops, and pushing ourselves to grow and learn about how best to educate in the twenty-first century.

Teaching from what we know about language and what we expect student writing to look like can be positive, as long as our lenses are global enough and generous enough to accept diverse skills, purposes, and products. But if we only lean on what I've described in the previous items, then we tend to stay safe and react to what we learned in our own school experience, or what we have been told by programs and publishers to look for.

Why the Old Lenses for Reading Student Writing No Longer Suffice

Most everyone who reads has noticed that many writers seem to defy the rules of grammar and organization. We all read a poem or two by e.e. cummings in high school, and invariably, our English teachers told us that cummings had something called "poetic license" for breaking rules of grammar and punctuation. Cummings might be the most obvious and famous rule breaker, but when you begin to study any kind of text for the author's style and structure, you see all sorts of infractions against what we thought were rules written in stone. Does that seem fair, we might ask, that we correct kids for mistakes that grown-up writers make with impunity?

Most people would say that fairness is not the issue here—learning correct or Standard Written English is. Probably the most frequent argument I hear from adults about why we must teach students the same kinds of grammatical rules and regulations that we learned is that "kids need to know the rules before they can break them." One danger in this proposition is that the rules we teach may be outdated. Now that we have pinpointed the places we heard, saw, and learned what we see and say about student writing, it's time to expose our knowledge for what it is: flawed. That's right—what we believe we know about error is often in error! No one is to blame for all this misunderstanding; remember, we teach what we learned. But perhaps if I lay out some eye-opening facts about what we learned, we might begin to adjust our lenses for reading student writing. Here are some problems with the "learn-the-rules-before-breaking-them" maxim:

- Rules change and more quickly than ever as digital literacies, such as text messaging, begin to dominate the ways people write.
- Rules vary according to discipline, purpose, audience, and genre. I studied journalism for four years, where I learned (the hard way, with punitive grades!) *not* to put commas before the *and* in a series, if there are more than three items: "discipline, purpose, audience and genre" (note: my copyeditor for this book tried to fix that sentence to fit Chicago style). In good old-fashioned (albeit disappearing) newspaper writing, where paper and ink are expensive, the more ways you can save space, the better. Not putting those pesky, unnecessary commas saves ink and column inches, and therefore lots of pieces of newsprint, in the long run.

It takes a bit of wrenching for me to pull away from what I learned in journalism classes so long ago—to write an entire article in an "inverted pyramid" format. Again, because of space constraints, the most important, hard-core facts had to appear in the first paragraph, preferably in the first sentence. Then, the information proceeds in order of steadily diminishing importance, with the least critical information in the very last paragraphs so that if inches are needed, these can be cut without losing the important details. As a speech, essay, and book writer, I now know that I want my endings to be the "amen" on whatever I write. I work perhaps hardest on the endings, and in fact, I cut out parts in the *middle* of my writing and cling to the ending as if it were a life preserver in the middle of an ocean.

- Rules vary according to publishing style. My thumb automatically bounces off the space bar two times at the ends of sentences. As a sophomore in high school, I was strictly trained, like a dog, with a ruler bouncing off my fingers and a C on my report card, to do so. Heinemann, the publishers of this very book I'm writing, asks that authors put only one space after the period, confusing and wrong to my thumb. I hear Mrs. So-and-so haranguing us, "Period, tap-tap; period, tap-tap."

Across the spectrum of creativity and invention are people who push against, if not utterly obliterate, the rules and conventions—teaching and testing to "mastery" leaves many students behind, sometimes literally, as they fail to pass into the next grade or to graduate.

Why Reach for a Wider Discourse About the Conventions of Writing?

- We can acknowledge and demonstrate that many types of writing exist in the world and teach that different disciplines, professions, purposes, and audiences affect the forms and conventions of texts. Doing so will cast a wider net to gather the interests and expertise of more kids doing more and different kinds of writing.
- We can offer a more authentic discourse about writing that reflects how all kinds of writers operate in our world and doesn't hold kids hostage in an educational system that in many ways has not changed during the last seventy-five years.
- We can liberate all children, but especially those who are second-, third-, or fourth-language learners, those who struggle whether for medical and/or mental and emotional issues, or who simply "don't fit" for any reasons whatsoever.
- We can encourage writing that will be read by real readers, who are more exacting and harder to please than any rules, rubrics, tests, or grades. If your best buddy can't read your new horror story without you beside her, telling her what it says, then you will want to know how to fix that.

The Good News: Celebrating Teachers of Writing

The good news about realizing that we need to change what we see and say to students about their writing is that the sources of information we have now are vast and easily accessible. Unlike the published writing programs I mentioned earlier in

Is There Ever a Time and Place for Demanding "Correct" Writing?

Yes. Some writing tasks demand a level of correctness in content, form, grammar, and readability. Some general examples:

- directions for using life-saving tools, such as fire extinguishers and heart defibrillators
- instruction manuals for operating potentially hazardous materials and machines

We do not want our brain surgeon or our airplane pilot learning how to remove tumors from our brains or land jet planes in the fog from poetry books. There are definitely instances when texts must pass rigorous standards of factual content knowledge and language conventionality. I would argue that a short story by a fifth grader or even an analytical essay about literature by a ninth grader are not texts that can or should be held to such rigid standards of correctness.

this chapter, these are resources provided by people who write and have researched how others write. They teach writing as a composing process, not as a list of isolated skills to plug into prefabricated sentences. They teach what it means to live wide-awake to the world and respond with a blog entry, a graphic novel, a poem, a feature article, or a play.

We should always be able to provide a comment that will lift the quality of any student's writing because the resources for teaching writing have multiplied dramatically over the last forty years. Since the 1970s, writing experts like Donald Murray, Donald Graves, Lucy Calkins, Randy Bomer, Nancie Atwell, Georgia Heard, Carl Anderson, Ralph Fletcher, JoAnn Portalupi, and Katie Wood Ray, among many others, have propelled us into a world awash with books, articles, speeches, workshop presentations, Internet sites, and DVDs about the qualities of good writing and how to teach them. Most teaching preparation courses at colleges and universities are at least familiar with the writing process, and many offer courses in how to teach writing workshop. Professional development organizations, such as the Teachers College

Reading and Writing Project, the National Council of Teachers of English, the National Writing Project, and numerous publishers and independent sources offer sustained professional development in writing, either through organized institutes and courses, or by offering onsite professional development from experienced consultants.

Also, as readers and writers ourselves, we actually know a great deal about what writing should look and sound like. I think teachers often downplay their knowledge and experience about what constitutes successful writing, perhaps thinking that school writing has to fit specific criteria on constrained rubrics, rather than remembering that good writing moves, entertains, informs, and calls to action. If we think of writing in those broader terms, we can rely on some of our own barometers as readers and writers of texts. It helps to remind ourselves frequently of what we know about good writing by thinking about these broad areas of influence.

What Do You Enjoy Reading?

When I present to groups of teachers about how to set up reading workshops in their classroom, I often begin by asking them what they read. At first, teachers are shy and answer with names of books by fancy and famous authors. Or they remain silent, perhaps thinking that I expect them to name William Faulkner or Emily Dickinson. Knowing this, I dig until teachers admit that they read political blogs online or Japanese manga, or they do genealogy research for their family tree, or that they read Patricia Cornwell every night before bed, or that they can't go to the beach without the latest book in the vampire romance series by Stephenie Meyer. They have subscriptions to *O Magazine* and they read do-it-yourself construction or cookbooks.

Why doesn't this count as reading? I ask. All of these texts contain lessons for teaching kids to write, and in fact, the more we know about these diverse text forms, the more we can tap into what kids are reading and help them draw connections for their own writing.

What Do You Enjoy Writing?

Many teachers I know write daily in notebooks or journals. Many keep active blogs online or write daily news updates on their Twitter or Facebook pages. Teachers have spoken movingly about letter writing giving them a reason to write and showing them a warm, immediate reader response they never got from any writing instruction in school. Some teachers publish articles in teaching magazines and journals, and still others belong to writing groups where they work on their own poetry, short stories, memoir, or other kinds of lifewriting. These are all sites and sources of writing instruction, I would argue. Whatever we do in our own writing process can provide specific, powerful lessons in writing for our students. I think we're sometimes afraid to reveal parts of our own process, for example, the fact that we procrastinate, borrow ideas from other writers, or worry about criticism from our readers. Yet, those are precisely the kinds of revelations into the writing process that kids want and need to know.

In the next few chapters, I will show you how to use your authentic reading and writing life to bring things to say to students about their writing.

3

What Can We Learn from Reading Widely in Modern Texts and Naming What We Admire?

Read, read, read. Read everything—trash, classics, good and bad, and see how they do it.
Just like a carpenter who works as an apprentice and studies the master. Read!
You'll absorb it. Then write. If it is good, you'll find out.

—WILLIAM FAULKNER

Hundreds of times, I have leaned in to students during a writing conference and whispered, "Do you want to know the secret to learning how to write?" They always say yes and then lean closer to hear it. I don't know what they expect the secret will be—a golden compass? A magic potion? Probably they think it will be something really boring like "Practice, practice, practice," as my piano teachers used to say, trying to sell me on the need to play scales for fifteen minutes every day.

But no. The true secret to learning how to write is to *read*. Read anything and everything: blogs, graphic novels, television scripts, legal briefs, magazine ad copy; all these texts have purposes, audiences, structures, and *lessons to learn* for a writer.

And now, would you like to know the secret to teaching how to write? *Read.* Read anything and everything: blogs, graphic novels, TV and movie scripts, magazine ads; all of these texts have purposes, audiences, structures, and *lessons to teach* a writer.

In gyms and locker rooms across the United States, football, basketball, and soccer players watch videos of winning teams and scoring plays in order to observe the moves that win games and trophies. Coaches play the videos in slow motion and instruct their players to study, frame-by-frame, second-by-second, the moves that high-scoring players make in order to learn from them. This kind of careful observation and naming of specific moves is a kind of reading. Rather than words, the players read actions. Rather than name literary terms or analyze text structures or interpret meanings of text, they name, analyze, and interpret the game plans and strategies of winning teams.

Apprentice painters famously prop their easels in front of master works in museums all over the world to study and imitate how to paint light, how to compose objects, how to make fabric look like fabric, how to imply physical motion, and how to make faces carry real emotion on canvas. In *Note by Note: A Celebration of the Piano Lesson*, Tricia Tunstall writes of her piano student who "needed a sound to imitate" (2008, 130) before he could find the emotion expressed in the passage of the Beethoven sonata he was trying to play. I believe that humans read the world in order to learn how to dress, walk, and act. When confronted with a new place or situation, such as buying a fare card to ride the Washington, DC, Metro train, or twisting into "pigeon pose" in yoga class, or eating with chopsticks, we look around at others to learn how things are done. When we want to build something, whether it's a bookshelf or a house, we look at other bookshelves and houses to study and borrow from the ones we like.

It's the same with writing. The world has published confessions from dozens of writers and poets, and behind those must be thousands of unpublished stories, of learning how to write from reading. Poet James Tate said he had to start from scratch when he went to college and wanted to learn to write poetry, so he went to the library and began to read work by poets. He knew he couldn't write like John Donne and didn't wish to write like Swinburne, so he turned to modern poets who

> shone the beacon of possibilities for a young, beginning poet setting forth. . . . [William Carlos] Williams told me there was a twentieth-century American language: you could hear it on the streets, and there was poetry there if one had the ear to hear it. Hart Crane was heartbreaking in his extreme passion for language and in his making of an American mythology. [Wallace] Stevens told me the imagination was boundless, and that it was okay to have fun with words and that fun could lead to insights and even profundities. . . . These poets—Williams, Crane, and Stevens—opened enough doors for a lifetime. (2000, 235)

Ah . . . poetry in the streets, if you have the ear to hear it! And poetry in child-hood nursery rhymes and jump-rope chants and hip-hop and popular songs. The oral and written texts that surround us become our writing teachers. When I was little, my mother read Bible stories to me, and in church every Sunday morning I heard the highly formal language of the liturgy and the cadences of hymns. Surely, the look and sound of those texts had some influence on my writing style. The first short story I wrote in seventh grade shared close similarities with the *Nancy Drew* mysteries I read when I was in elementary school.

My first poems, written when I was about fifteen, were lonely, untutored, but conscious efforts to write like the chiefs and tribal women and men in an anthology of Native American writings called *Touch the Earth* (McLuhan 1971). Those writings became my teachers; I wanted to write like the chiefs and warriors of the Ottawan and Chippewa tribes and like Chief Joseph of the Nez Perces. One of my favorite passages was from an old holy Wintu woman who spoke about the destruction by gold mining of the land where she lived: "We don't chop down the trees. We only use dead wood. But the White people plow up the ground, pull down the trees, kill everything. The tree says, 'Don't. I am sore. Don't hurt me. . . .' Everywhere the White man has touched [the earth] it is sore" (1971, 15).

In my little green spiral notebook, and for my eyes only, I tried to capture that sense of the earth being hurt. I wrote my poem from the point of view of a native medicine man leaning against a telephone pole, the only "man-made" object (a sym-bol of relentlessly encroaching technology and civilization) in a snow-covered plain, in a painting I had seen, by Henry F. Farny called *Song of the Talking Wire*.

Talking Wires

I lean my sorrow against this dead tree and listen
to voices singing through wires.
They say they are coming soon,
riding on iron monsters
along tracks that cut
and scar the land forever.

I believe it was during those sessions of reading and imitating while tucked away in the closet of my bedroom that I became a poet. Truth be told, I fantasized that I had been adopted from the Dine (also known as Navajo) because I felt such a strong kinship with the idea of nature being a living, breathing, sentient being. The themes and language of those native writings still echo in my prose and poetry.

Informing Our Eyes and Ears

As teachers, we can learn a great deal about writing, not from how-to texts, and certainly not from content-less rubric categories, or lists of isolated literary terms, but from actual poems, articles, novels, scripts, songs, and essays, as well as newer forms of texts such as graphic novels and electronic texts: blogs, zine articles, wikis, email, Twitter, and text messaging. If we read a lot of contemporary texts, we will develop an eye and ear for how language is used *now*, not one hundred years ago. Language and genre or text forms evolve over time and with the needs and purposes of groups of people. The way English was written and spoken in 1590 only vaguely resembles the look and sound of modern English.

Consider the spellings and word choice in this sample stanza from a poem many of us sweated over in high school, "The Faerie Queene," by Sir Edmund Spenser (See? Right off the bat—the spelling of *fairy* has changed quite a bit, and *queen* no longer has a silent *e* at the end.):

> Then listen Lordings, if ye list to weet
> > The cause, why Satyrane and Paridell
> > Mote not be entertaynd, as seemed meet,
> > Into that Castle (as that Squire does tell).
> > "Therein a cancred crabbéd Carle does dwell,
> > That has no skill of Court nor courtesie,
> > Ne cares, what men say of him ill or well;
> > For all his dayes he drownes in privitie,
> Yet has full large to live, and spend at libertie.
> (Book III, Canto IX)

What? Spenser's spelling alone practically made smoke come out of my computer's spell-check feature! And my Norton's *Anthology of Poetry* has to supply meanings to many of Spenser's words in the margins because these words have fallen from our lexicon: *weet* (know); *Mote* (may); *Carle* (*churl*, which word, by the way, has never been uttered by anyone in earshot my whole life), and *privitie* (*seclusion*, which I might have been able to infer from the similarity to *private*, but which sounds like what my Oklahoma farming family called an outhouse).

Obviously, spellings and word meanings have changed, and will continue to change, despite the grousing of many who wish it would just stand still and be constantly *correct*. But also syntax and diction have changed; the high tone exists no longer. Even in poems written for the most formal of occasions, words flow in different ways now. Compare Sir Edmund Spenser's language with that of the beautiful poem "Praise Song for the Day," written by Elizabeth Alexander for President Barack Obama's inauguration in 2009 (this poem is easily available on the Internet). Alexander's words are simple, about the uncelebrated work and lives of most Americans, and about the history of those who have suffered injustices in our country. She even writes movingly at one point in the poem: "Say it plain: that many have died for this day." Though it is a poem, the syntax sounds more like the way we talk, certainly, than Spenser's. And the topics that are possible to write about now, in the infancy of the twenty-first century—the life situations, cultural histories, and human conditions that this poem and others reveal—have opened up dramatically.

Changes in the way written texts look and sound have occurred so rapidly in the last few decades, many of us can hardly keep up. But we must try. The more we can dip into contemporary and diverse texts, the more we can feed our eyes and ears with the shapes and sounds that writers use today. We do students a terrible disservice if we expect them to write like Milton, when the texts they read and listen to sound more like jazz or hip-hop and look like comics, animation, and colorful websites.

Reading Published Texts with a Writer's Eye and Ear

Let's look at a few adult texts to learn how to reframe our reading toward some large features of writing style and away from language conventions. The more often we practice doing this, the broader our concepts will be for how texts look and sound, and the more vocabulary we will develop for teaching writing. The most enjoyable way to do this work is with a partner or better yet, with a small reading group. Many eyes on a piece of writing can yield bushels of ideas. All you need are some friends and colleagues and some short, shared texts: poems, short stories, essays, feature articles, blogs, or excerpts from novels and longer nonfiction books. Oh, and you'll need notebooks, pens, highlighters, chart paper, or perhaps worksheets to fill out with all your findings, such as the T-chart examples that follow later in this chapter (blank charts are provided in Appendix B).

Noticing and Naming Elements of Style in Published Adult Texts

First, read a short text or an excerpt from a longer text silently or out loud to a partner or in a small group. Next, write for five minutes in response to the following protocol (also found in Appendix A) for reading texts that I've modified from a protocol devised by Randy Bomer. Then, share your responses with your partner or group.

General Protocol for Reading Published Texts

1. Respond initially to what this text says to you—what it reminds you of from your own life; what it makes you think about; what surprises you and pleases you aesthetically.

2. Point to places where you think the writing is "good." A place that stuns you—one that you almost wish you had written yourself. If possible, mark those places with circles, underlines, stars, margin notes, or use sticky notes if you can't physically mark the text.

3. Describe simply and plainly (don't label with literary terms) what the writer is doing. Even if you struggle to figure out exactly how to name this technique, describing the text will help you dig into writing craft better than slapping a label on it. You may write about how that part affects you as a reader. Push yourself to let go of all those terms you learned in school, like *simile* and *alliteration*, and try to name what the effect of that comparison or sound has on you. For instance, instead of "it's *sequenced*," try something like "I can follow the character minute-by-minute

as the events unfold—as if I'm with her walking along that strip of beach, waiting for news of how the hunt went and if anyone was hurt."

4. List your responses, or fill out charts with the groups' ideas that you can then take to your own classroom to use as *cheat sheets* for responding to your student's writing. You can decide to simply list a bit of text you admire in one column and how you think the author did that in the second column. Or you can use charts such as the ones you see filled out later in this chapter to focus on one of the qualities of good writing that often appear on writing rubrics, such as Voice and Structure (see Appendix B). (See Chapter 4 for more ideas about how to crack open the rubric labels in order to describe the qualities of writing more specifically to your students.)

In my summer writing institute course at Teachers College Reading and Writing Project, we practiced looking at published texts together for several days using this reading protocol. At first, it was a bit of a struggle to name admired places without using the literary terms we all know and love—*personification* and *simile*—or the handy rubric words that we're required to use when preparing our students for state writing tests—*organization* and *details*. But I kept pushing everyone's thinking (I hope they forgave me!), and soon enough, people were sounding like poets and literary theorists and artists as they sought to describe how the texts affected them as readers. In many instances, I could tell that teachers were fans of Katie Wood Ray's *Wondrous Words* because I heard her delicious names for things (*close echo, whispering parenthesis, seesaw sentences*) applied to the new texts I presented. I encourage you to use Katie's labels because they are so much more descriptive than *voice* and *organization*. The trick, I knew, would be finding and using those lovely phrases when we looked at *student* writing, especially writing about gangs or video games or writing that was nearly impossible to read through all the glaring errors. But we will get to that part of the story in Chapter 6.

What follows are excerpts from just a smattering of the texts I've used in workshops with teachers. Following them, I've included some of the teachers' brilliant naming for different aspects they noticed and admired in the texts.

"What We Talk About When We Talk About Love" by Raymond Carver

The group of teachers read the entire Carver short story, but this little excerpt gives you a taste of the text. The whole story takes place around a kitchen table, as three couples drink themselves silly and talk about what love is and is not. In this example, we simply followed the reading protocol and then listed our overall responses to this text:

> My friend Mel McGinnis was talking. Mel McGinnis is a cardiologist, and sometimes that gives him the right.
>
> The four of us were sitting around his kitchen table drinking gin. Sunlight filled the kitchen from the big window behind the sink. There were Mel and me and his second wife, Teresa—Terri, we called her—and my wife, Laura. We lived in Albuquerque then. But we were all from somewhere else.
>
> There was an ice bucket on the table. The gin and the tonic water kept going around, and we somehow got on the subject of love. Mel thought real love was nothing less than spiritual love. He said he'd spent five years in a seminary before quitting to go to medical school. He said he still looked back on those years in the seminary as the most important years in his life.
>
> Terri said the man she lived with before she lived with Mel loved her so much he tried to kill her. Then Terri said, "He beat me up one night. He dragged me around the living room by my ankles. He kept saying, 'I love you, I love you, you b—.' He went on dragging me around the living room. My head kept knocking on things." Terri looked around the table. "What do you do with love like that?"
>
> She was a bone-thin woman with a pretty face, dark eyes, and brown hair that hung down her back. She liked necklaces made of turquoise, and long pendant earrings.
>
> "My God, don't be silly. That's not love, and you know it," Mel said. "I don't know what you'd call it, but I sure know you wouldn't call it love." (1982, 137–38)

Teachers' Responses

- First person (*I*) helps us be a voyeur on this conversation.
- A physicality (dragging around, head knocking on things). Tactile words.

- Uses very ordinary, everyday language.
- He uses *said* every time someone says something, and you don't notice it at all. He doesn't need *proclaimed* or *exclaimed* because what comes out of the characters' mouths is what's important.
- Goes from narration to dialogue, narration to dialogue, it's like a jolt each time because both are so short.
- Reader is like a witness to people out of control, coming undone before our eyes.
- The title sounds like a self-help book, but the story makes you completely depressed about what love is like in modern times!
- Bases a character on a stereotype so that reader builds theory about that character in very few words (e.g., a *cardiologist*, a heart doctor, perfect choice for a story about love!).
- Makes characters talk like the kind of [stereotypical] persons they are.

The Brief Wondrous Life of Oscar Wao by Junot Díaz

This novel won the Pulitzer Prize in 2007. I deeply admire this novel, as well as Díaz's first book, *Drown*. In *The Brief Wondrous Life*, Díaz creates a mash-up of fiction and facts about the Dominican Republic, humor and brutality, English and Spanish. He footnotes inside fiction, so you wonder, *is that* really *a fact?*, and he includes so many allusions to pop culture and science fiction that I often had no clue what I was reading. It helped to read this little excerpt with a group, as we did in the summer institute section because many pair of eyes revealed the richness embedded in just one page.

> You should have seen him, his mother sighed in her Last Days. He was our Little *Porfirio Rubriosa*. [That name had a half page footnote attached in the text.]
>
> All the other boys his age avoided the girls like they were a bad case of Captain Trips. Not Oscar. The little guy loved himself the females, had "girl-friends" galore. (He was a stout kid, heading straight to fat, but his mother kept him nice in haircuts and clothes, and before the proportions of his head changed he'd had these lovely flashing eyes and these cute-ass cheeks, visible in all his pictures.) The girls—his sister Lola's friends, his mother's friends, even their neighbor, Mari Colon, a thirty-something postal employee who wore red on her lips and walked like she had a bell for an ass—all purportedly fell for him. *Ese muchacho esta bueno!* (Did it hurt that he was earnest and clearly

attention-deprived? Not at all!) In the DR during summer visits to his family digs in Bani he was the worst, would stand in front of Nena Inca's house and call out to passing women—*Tu eres guapa! Tu eres guapa!*—until a Seventh-day Adventist complained to his grandmother and she shut down the hit parade lickety-split. *Muchacho del Diablo!* This is not a cabaret! (2007, 12–13)

Teachers' Responses

Kind of Voice	*How Does Author Do That?*
Teenlike	Slang; "situated" (cultural) language, incomplete sentences; real kid issues
Intellectual	Footnotes (in a novel!); dense text; long, meandering sentences
Political, irreverent	Historical background; obscure references
Sarcastic, mocking, angry	Straightforward language; cussing
Witty, purposefully clever	Self-created words; intimate words; references to pop culture (video games, science fiction)

"Unhappy Meals" by Michael Pollan

This was originally a feature article that appeared in *The New York Times Magazine* in 2007 and, in 2009, became a nonfiction book called *In Defense of Food: An Eater's Manifesto.*

Michael Pollan is one my favorite nonfiction writers. His prose sings with poetry; his voice is often sarcastic and biting. He writes with urgency about topics I care a great deal about: the earth, biology, and food.

Eat food. Not too much. Mostly plants.

That, more or less, is the short answer to the supposedly incredibly complicated and confusing question of what we humans should eat in order to be maximally healthy. I hate to give away the game right here at the beginning of a long essay, and I confess that I'm tempted to complicate matters in the interest of keeping things going for a few thousand more words. I'll try to resist but will go ahead and add a couple more details to flesh out the advice. Like: A little meat won't kill you, though it's better approached as a side dish than as a main. And you're much better off eating whole fresh foods than processed food products. That's what I mean by the recommendation to eat "food." Once, food was all you could eat, but today there are lots of other edible foodlike substances in the supermarket. These novel products of food science often come in packages festooned with health claims, which brings me to a related rule of thumb: if you're concerned about your health, you should probably avoid food products that make health claims. Why? Because a health claim on a food product is good indication that it's not really food, and food is what you want to eat. (1)

Teachers' Responses

Structure	*How Does Author Do That?*
Fun ride!	Timing of a stand-up comedian
	Juxtaposes sentence and para-
	graph lengths: short, long
Combination "how-to" and	Direct "do this/do that," followed
"why-to"	by a scientific explanation
Circular journey	First words repeat in last sentence
Zooms in, focuses instantly	First paragraph says it all

"Where Is the Love?" by June Jordan

June Jordan was a poet, essayist, memoirist, and political activist. Her essays remind me of boiling water; they bubble and burst forth, often in almost spitting anger. They certainly do not fit anything like a five-paragraph, or accordion paragraphs or any other formula for essay writing. They do take an idea on a journey of thought, which is my favorite description of what an essay, and a blog, can do.

As a Black woman/feminist, I must look about me, with trembling, and with shocked anger, at the endless waste, the endless suffocation of my sisters: the bitter sufferings of hundreds of thousands of women who are the sole parents, the mothers of hundreds of thousands of children, the desolation and the futility of women trapped by demeaning, lowest-paying occupations, the unemployed, the bullied, the beaten, the battered, the ridiculed, the slandered, the trivialized, the raped, and the sterilized, the lost millions and multimillions of beautiful, creative, and momentous lives turned to ashes on the pyre of gender identity. I must look about me and, as a Black feminist, I must ask myself: Where is the love? How is my own lifework serving to end these tyrannies, these corrosions of sacred possibility? (2002, 272)

Teachers' Responses

- "Raging" words.
- Long sentences and lots of commas give it a hurried quality.
- That list of brutal nouns pounds you, the reader, over the head.
- The title shocks reader to attention.
- Repetition, "I must look about me, I must look about me, I must look behind me," reminds me of "I Have a Dream" speech by Martin Luther King Jr.

Various Essays by Lisa Kogan

In the summer institute group, we tried to decipher Kogan's techniques for humorous writing. Kogan is a monthly columnist for *O Magazine* and writes often wickedly funny observations on life in these times. To me, humor is the hardest kind of writing to pull off, and though not every paragraph that Kogan writes works every time, she frequently elicits LOL (laughing out loud) when I read her essays with teachers. Here are some strategies we decided Kogan uses:

- Takes everyday, small, simple things and blows them up, cranks them up to absurdity.
- Lists several examples (usually three) to describe what she means, each more outrageous than the last.
- Not caring who reads this; like talking to a friend; not afraid to write like you write in your diary, like no one is looking, and you're saying what you *have* to say.
- No filter!
- Writing in the real-time moment, like an open document she's typing into. Like language and a thought bubble up at the same time.
- Deadpan tone.
- An intentional, sarcastic use of three exclamation marks!!!

Noticing and Naming Elements of Style in Everyday Texts

Over the years, I've used piles of examples of everyday texts: ads, billboards, instruction manuals, greeting cards, recipes, cereal boxes, museum placards, playbills, business letters, junk mail, game manuals, and more as examples of qualities of good writing. Truly, if we open our eyes, great writing is everywhere we look. I copy these texts and use them with teachers and kids, and we read and analyze them using the same reading protocol described earlier. While I have files full of examples, I love pulling out whatever text is literally on my kitchen counter or computer screen to prove that there's not one perfect text, but rather that we can apply the reading protocol to whatever is in front of our faces. At the time of writing, the following two texts (besides this book) were facing me.

Not Answering Calls

And what if you're listening to a *really* good song, or you see that the call comes from someone you *really* don't want to deal with right now?

In that case, you have two choices. First, you can just ignore it. If you wait long enough (four rings), the call will go to voicemail (even if you've silenced the ring/vibrating as described above).

Second, you can dump it to voicemail *immediately* (instead of waiting for the four rings). How you do that depends on the set up . . .

. . . Of course, if your callers know you have an iPhone, they'll also know that you've deliberately dumped them into voicemail—because they won't hear all four rings. (Pogue 2008, 39)

David Pogue is a tech columnist for *The New York Times,* and the author of a whole series of *Missing Manuals*—how-tos for software and electronics. He uses *really,* twice (his English teacher would have winced), and even emphasizes it with italics. His sentences are short and mostly in the subject-verb structure, nothing fancy. Pogue's voice is sarcastic, witty, and extremely thoughtful and clear. It's as if he can read your mind and know what confuses you about technology. And he doesn't talk down to you either—a nice touch in a manual for the technophobic.

Omni Group Website: www.omnigroup.com

There's more to our bookmarks than just being able to save your favorite web-sites. Oh yes. MUCH more. We'd tell you, but then we'd have to kill you.

Or not. What, is this web page gonna whap you in the head, or something? Anyway, ahem—bookmarks. So! OmniWeb's bookmarks are more powerful than ever, with filtered views of bookmarks and history that lets you easily see your most visited web sites or all the bookmarked pages that have been updated since you last visited them.

Doesn't it seem like the Omni Group would be a blast to work for? This company builds software applications for Mac computers, and its website is a delight to behold: beautifully designed, colorful, and *easy* to navigate. The voice in this text sounds like the kind of smart-alecky kids I was attracted to in high school—the type who now write for the fake newspaper, *The Onion*. "We'd tell you, but then we'd have to kill you." HA!

But seriously, beyond the fun, this prose does the work of instructing and explaining with panache. It catches your attention instantly, makes you giggle, makes you relax, makes you want to read on about, and probably purchase, electronic bookmarks.

How to Help Students Read Like Writers

The same protocol and techniques for reading texts like writers can easily be applied to texts, for any age or grade level, that you and your students read in the classroom. When I teach students from kindergarten to college how to read texts like writers, I've used the same reading protocol I suggested teachers use alongside published texts. As a class, we read short texts or excerpts from longer works together, first to enjoy, argue with, and relate to what the text says. Next, we point to places where we admire the writing technique, and then we talk about what the writer is doing in those places, using language that attempts to name how it affects us as readers, talking long, stumbling over ourselves to name something the writer does without just pushing it into a tidy box labeled with a literary term.

With older students, I can ask them to fill out the T-charts just as the teachers do in my summer institute sections. I have nothing against using literary terminology in the process of learning about writing technique as long as I feel my students understand what a term means and what effect it has on the reader. I do not make a list of terms to memorize or quiz kids on the difference between *metaphor* and *simile*. Being able to shout out "that's a synecdoche!" sounds mighty impressive coming from a sixth grader, but the deeper question I want students to answer is "what is it doing there?" What effect does using a part to stand for the whole have (e.g., count *heads* to see if we have every *person* present) on the reader?

At the beginning of any genre study, I spend from three to five days with students reading and talking about published texts in the genre we are about to write. As an example, for a poetry study, I cut and paste dozens of poems and copy them into packets for each student. I purposely choose poems written in the last twenty years or so, and I select ones that dispel some old-fashioned notions of what poetry is, for instance that it's "about nature and love; it rhymes; it's boring." I copy poems about cities, families, garbage, cats, fear, history, loss, and physical pain, and none of them rhyme, at least at the beginning of our study.

I prepare in the same way for prose studies, finding at least five short samples of fiction or nonfiction and I either make copies for each student or put the sample up on the overhead, LCD projector, or document camera so that we can look at the text together as a class. For longer texts, like memoir or longer fiction and nonfiction, I excerpt small sections to copy and study.

When we study texts together in the writing workshop minilesson, I first read the piece out loud and then ask students to talk with a partner about what they notice. As often as possible, I want kids to talk about writing using language that they can understand and that is meaningful to them. Remember in high school (oh, poor old high school keeps getting bruised by my discouraging words, doesn't it?), when we studied poetry, many of us experienced something like this: teacher hands out a sheet (mimeographed in my day; that intoxicating smell!) with ten to twenty elements and subgenres of poetry and their definitions—*alliteration, iambic pentameter, assonance, metaphor* and *simile* (remember trying to memorize the difference?), *stanza, trope, epic, lyrical, ballad, ode,* and all the rest. In contrast, in a writing workshop genre study, kids read, talk about, dissect, and circle around the poems *first*, then come up with meaningful, fanciful, and fantastic language to explain what poets do in poems.

Kate Kuonen, a wickedly smart and innovative teacher in Indianapolis, prepared her fifth and sixth graders to respond to writers' craft so well all year long, that they brought an ease and skill to their study of songwriting. A sixth grader named Tiana, looking at a song with her reading group, said the writer was making something a *disguise*. "Songs use a 'disguise,' like 'The Long Train' means something else besides a train that's long. You know, like trying to put a mask on it and not say what it really is." Tiana was describing a metaphor, but other kids in the group instantly understood her idea about disguise, and that became the way that class explained when a writer is comparing something to something else. A student in my own fourth- and fifth-grade class said he liked the way the mountains were like a friend to the little girl; they breathed and they comforted her when she was sad. Even though he was describing personification, the kids referred to "Daniel's mountain" whenever they wanted to make an inanimate object come alive in their writing.

We continue this work of looking together at texts as models of whatever genre we are creating for about a week. After reading a text together in the minilesson, the kids work with partners or in groups of three and four to look at more samples of whatever genre we're studying. In their writer's notebooks, they list more places in the texts where they admire how a writer has arranged words, structured time, entered a character's mind, or painted the scenery (a fourth grader's way of naming setting!). These lists of literary devices become the guidebook for kids' own writing when they begin to compose. The language the class develops to name how texts are built not only instructs students' composing processes but it also finds its way into the ways that kids talk about their process to me in conferences and in peer conferences and peer writing groups. As you can imagine, this rich dialogue about the craft of writing both gives and takes from discussions during reading workshop as well.

Reading Student Writing the Way We Read Published Texts

My friend, Barbara Clements, is a breathtakingly intelligent and reflective fifth- and sixth-grade teacher in Washington, DC. She reads and writes constantly, so her expectations for what texts look and sound like are informed and sophisticated. Like all great teachers, she has high expectations for her students' writing because she has witnessed them in the writer's workshop meeting and exceeding her expectations year after year. Also, like all of us, she sometimes feels disappointed about the disconnect between the high-level understandings her students seem to have when they *talk* about writing during minilessons and the actual written texts they produce. Barbara reflected on that problem in an email message to me one day. Her insightful and poetic words just stunned me, and she kindly gave me permission to print them here.

Reflections on Our Writer's Workshop by Barbara Clements

I pore over the writing my students have done this year, and I'm impressed by the volume of their writing. They have filled writer's notebooks, they have written personal narratives, a personal essay, a short story and poetry. They have written book reviews and short essays. But, as I begin reading their pieces, I begin to doubt myself. The work seemed better when they were writing it— what happened to the excitement I felt at the time?

I read more carefully and begin to find the bits and pieces I was impressed with. I read Molly's piece about her family and am immediately drawn in by the words: "One evening in the mountains, as it started getting dark. . . ."

I see the potential Leo has to be a sensitive writer in his poems about Bethany Beach:

> As the sun sets
> And the town of Bethany readies for bed,
> My friends and I play on a darkening beach.
> As day ends,
> And night begins
> We enter the twilight zone.
> Parents shout but we don't hear them
> All we hear is the pounding of the surf
> And the slapping of our feet against the sand.

What a far cry from his blow-by-blow accounts of football games that dominated his narratives.

I smile at Zoe's similes: "the millions and trillions of small blades of grass like grains of sand in the ocean, flowers like colorful fish in the sea. . . ." I sense Zoe's joy of life in her poem about a field of wildflowers.

These bits and pieces are jewels, some waiting to be set into a bigger whole, some waiting to be polished, their makers waiting for someone to show them how do to this.

What Barbara did, as she read her students' work, was to *change her stance* as a reader. She moved away from her first impulse to see what is missing or not living up to her expectations. She rejected herself becoming what Robert Probst calls an "opponent sparring in a linguistic ring, where students are attempting to slip confusions and inadequacies past the teacher, and the teacher [is] attempting to catch, label, and castigate all the flaws" (1989, 70).

Instead, Barbara became "impressed" by the writing, and began to "read more carefully." She was "immediately drawn in," "proud," and could "see the potential." And most important, she saw the "jewels" inside their pieces "waiting to be polished."

How can we all become such respectful readers of our students' writing? What will help all of us see the jewels in even the shortest, most poorly spelled and punctuated piece of writing we've ever encountered?

We need to do as Barbara did; we need to change our stance as readers, and we need new lenses (a new pair of reading glasses perhaps?) for looking at student writing. Gaby Layden, my friend and fellow literacy consultant who does deep, reflective work with students and teachers all over the United States, suggests that as adults with years of life experience and exposure to different kinds of text, we can and must read student writing with the "eye of possibility" for what is there and what it can become.

I love Gaby's phrase—"eye of possibility"—and I have suggestions for how we can look through that eye instead of the "eye of error" or whatever is the opposite of possibility. First, we need to read knowing that a student is trying to compose *meaning* on the page. Reading visionary, Marie Clay, urged reading teachers to remark on the "partially correct" in children's reading, rather than what is missing or wrong (Johnston 2004, 13). Can we flip that idea to writing? Can we remark on the "partially correct," the almost there, or what Peter Johnston calls the "leading edge of what is going well"? For, Johnston says, "this is the launching pad for new learning" (13). Can we notice that a student has written six fabulous sentences so far, rather than leaping to the need to elaborate, that actually the fact that she has nailed the experience of grief in only six sentences could be considered a mature restraint rather than something missing? Can we notice that a writer who loves re-creating video games in her notebook could potentially become a fabulous fantasy or science fiction writer?

Next, as I wrote in my Introduction, we need to read in a way that respects kids' writing, the way we would approach a new memoir by David Sedaris, anticipating that the work will be great, and will move us and make us laugh. We need to dig and inquire into student writing the way we would have to spend time with Spenser's "Faerie Queene," perhaps knowing we won't get the meaning right away—that we might have to read it a few times, and talk about it with someone else, so that our interpretations can begin to unfold. I urge all of us to spread out our students' writing, as my friend Barbara did, and read it like an artist.

As a little girl in the 1960s, I never missed watching a segment from the CBS show, *Art Linkletter's House Party*, called "Kids Say the Darndest Things." Kids sat in chairs on a platform, and Linkletter walked from one to the next, asking questions about everything under the sun. The hook of this show revolved around the fresh, naive, and therefore, funny or even wise-sounding ways that kids talk. Art Linkletter was like a gentle, loving father, amazed and sweetly amused by kids' answers. His show was wildly popular, and broadcast five days a week on radio and television for twenty-six years, with over 20,000 kid interviews. Linkletter may have been the first, perhaps the only person to bring children to the public's attention, proclaiming, in effect, "Hey, kids are smart and funny!" We need to bring that attitude to our reading of students' writing—expecting that there will be lines and whole chunks of text that will make us laugh, inspire us, and yes, even make us jealous. I've often said to kids—if you don't publish that image or story idea, I'm gonna steal it! They usually beam and say, "You can just take it, Ms. Bomer! For free!"

I propose a different list of things to look for in children's writing besides what we see first—the errors and what's missing—a different rubric if you will, to place beside their blossoming pieces. What I love to read has honesty, significance, and especially, unusual, surprising ways of saying things. I try to look at what the writer is doing, what features pop out, and how they affect me as a reader. Every student is doing something with his words, making some kind of meaning, and we can see it and name it for him.

In Chapters 4 and 5, I list dozens of examples of artful language for naming the beauty and brilliance in student writing. In Chapters 6 and 7, I demonstrate this kind of reading using several samples of student writing; but for now, let me implore that we learn how to change our stance as readers, and that we grant student texts the same time and respect we would give any other text published on paper or online. As this chapter has suggested, the more we read what people have been writing over the last few decades and especially what people are publishing in print and online to the joy of thousands and thousands of readers right this second, the more our eyes and ears will be primed for the influences our students feel, and we can celebrate their learning how to write from reading.

4

How Can We Use New Language to Effectively Speak to Kids About Quality in Writing?

Kids are almost as good as William Faulkner at telling stories. If you can wade through all the run-on sentences, there's a hidden treasure there, and good teachers know to begin there for motivation."

—JONATHAN KOZOL, NCTE address, 2007

At Box Gallery in Santa Fe, New Mexico, gallery owner Michelle Ouellette spoke about the contemporary artists she represents as if they were her own children, who could do no wrong, whose every dot of paint, every impulsive choice of paper/canvas/oil/clay was conceived in intuitive genius, enabling the artist to discover new territories and create new masterpieces. She took us on a tour of her current exhibitions, commenting on each treasure with poetic, exuberant language. I followed her from painting to painting, completely entranced. She spoke of one painter exploring *surface* when the oil paint stood out from the canvas in huge globs, sometimes including the scabs formed on oil tubes left open in the air, as well as any materials blowing about in the open-air studio the painter worked in, such as dust and leaves.

Michelle offered interpretations of the paintings, seeing things in them that I was blind to, opening my perceptions so that I began to fall madly in love with everything in the gallery, although at first, I found some of it strange and unattractive, or frightening. In one painting, called *With a Little Night Music,* by Kathleen Morris, Michelle invited me to notice that the girl was not bound by the black circles around her body, but rather *embraced* by them, *ensconced* in them. These were not ropes after all, but *wisps of smoke*, perhaps, encircling her. The hands were still and *at peace* in her lap. And she was *singing*—not screaming—the corners of her lips upturned in exaltation, not terror. Her hair was not ravaged but floating in some heavenly gel.

Randy and I spent an hour in that petite gallery, walking about with Michelle, and the words that she used to describe each piece of art—*tactile, wispy imaginings, verdant green, insides of night lights, bedazzled by landscape*—swirled in my head and transported me to another world, a world of enhanced and transformative beauty. Her ways of seeing made me look differently at the world, the dirt and railroad tracks and glaring sun that we stepped back out into. All the world was Art—open to my interpretive gaze and evocative, eloquent language, if I could only choose to see and say it that way. I tell you what, if Randy hadn't been there to protect our bank account, I might have put several paintings on the credit card that day and wondered later what had possessed me.

I want to be able to see such richness in art when I look at it and to talk in such keen, elegiac language as Michelle uses. And I want to be able to do the same for student writing, which might, like contemporary art, at first look or sound unattractive, odd, or wrong. Unfortunately, because of tests, state (soon to be federal) standards, and rubrics that create boxes for students to fit into, we seem to lean on the clunkiest ways to talk about writing and fall back on those lessons we were taught decades ago, many of which no longer apply. My hope is to take some of the more overused categories for talking about student writing—*voice, vocabulary, organization, details*, and *conventions*, and especially to take those ugly, evaluative labels, like *meets standard*—and try to move us away from those sterile descriptions toward a more tactile, more elegant, and certainly more enlivening language for writing.

Sometimes I think I should carry a cheat sheet of words *not* to use in a writing conference. I want to crack open words that echo school talk, like *vocabulary* and *sequencing*, or words that I never understood until college, like *audience*. (What audience? I would ask myself. Are we in a movie theatre, a rock concert? My only audience is my teacher and his red pen.) Instead, I want to talk to young writers as a person who loves to read a lot of different things. I try to speak as my friends and I do about books and writing, using the language of our trade. We might say something like, "I see this place you're describing so well, that I could probably paint it right now, in color." Or, "You keep your definitions lean, almost approaching a sound bite" (Thorpe 2001).

Now, you might be thinking, that's a long string of words, when *setting* or *clarity*, would do just as well. Well, yes. It is a long string of words because I think we need *long language,* to talk about language. In fact, it probably will take longer to respond to kids' writing than we're currently giving it when we use one-word labels like *organization* and *voice.* While we might need that jargon occasionally as shorthand when we talk to each other, we should try not to use it with kids. We need concrete, material, muscular talk in our classrooms; we need as many metaphors to teach something as we can, so that different kids can find their way into the complex and abstract world of writing composition.

Cracking Open the Top Six Writing Rubric Words

In this next section I offer some ways to talk long about the kind of labels and categories that appear on checklists and writing rubrics in school districts across the United States. I'm picking on assessment categories specifically for several reasons. First, in the name of speed and efficiency, the language that describes quality writing gets boiled down to one or two words to encompass acres of possibility. While this makes sense for evaluation purposes, these labels cannot begin to name the myriad talents and techniques that writers possess, nor can they provide meaningful instruction for young writers reaching out for concrete demonstrations of the look and sound of texts. Second, because one-word labels are tidy and simple, they have grown monstrously into what amounts to a writing curriculum for many overwhelmed teachers and comprise the vocabulary with which teachers and students communicate with each other about the practice of writing.

The assessment categories are, absolutely, what most people would agree a piece of good writing possesses, but they cannot begin to tease out the nuances of language or texts, or help students to understand what they already have or may continue to need in their writing. I have pulled these words from various state standards lists and writing rubrics. These words have been around a long time, and when Vicki Spandel (2001) explains in *Creating Writers* about how they came to be part of different standards guides and writing rubrics, she traces the extensive research, gathered over decades by many committees, who have read more than their share of student essays in order to come to consensus about what makes writing good. I agree with Spandel that when we teach, and especially when we assess students, we need to have a vision of what makes writing good, and then we need to make clear to students what we are looking for in their work. Ultimately, Spandel argues, we must turn that vision over to our students so that they can internalize the look and sound of good writing and revise their own drafts accordingly. I recommend reading *Creating Writers* for a thoughtful, knowledgeable, and engaging discussion of writing assessment. As with other bodies of work of visionary literacy educators, I believe that Spandel's contributions have become packaged and watered down so that school district mandates to "teach the *6 Trait writing*" substitute for the authentic, daily workings of a community of writers.

I have never felt that checklists or rubric categories, while conceivably useful as scoring guides for district and statewide writing assessments, can name writing quality for our students in ways that speak to them, that seem like we are talking about Art rather than jargon for graded and scored schoolwork. Mary Dentrone, a magnificent literacy coach at PS 199 in New York City, noticed that when she shifts the way she talks about writing to a more artful vocabulary, the students' writing noticeably reflects that. Mary read some before-and-after pieces and realized that "elevating my language in writing conferences leads to more elevated language in students' writing!" The language on state standards and rubrics for state tests use labels such as *Voice*, *Details*, and *Organization*. These flat, one-word rubric categories come to dictate how we respond to our students' writing, so in our harried teaching days, we end up telling them, for instance, that they need to write with voice, without instructing how or why to do that and without using concrete examples from texts. *Voice* is a concept that even adult writers argue about and name alternately *style*, *tone*, and *mood*, so how can we expect kids to understand it? To make matters worse, our rubrics measure kids' voice on a numerical scale, as in "You have a Number 2 voice," further abstracting the concept of what it takes to make writing sing.

Of course, we do want students to learn how to write in ways that engage readers, and voice plays an enormous role in that. But I think we can crack open concepts such as voice to name something specific from a student's writing and say it with words a writer or artist would use, using a lot of language to talk about language. We might say something such as, "Your writing voice is tense and edgy—kind of like your words are gritting their teeth, as if they want to be somewhere else, anywhere but here on this piece of paper."

When I *talk long*, I wrap a lot of language around what I notice and appreciate in student writing. I first name, with a muscular or juicy adjective, the specific *kind* of voice a piece of writing has—*compassionate, tyrannical, snide, ironic, cynical, pompous, cranky* (think Andy Rooney on *60 Minutes*). All words on paper have voice, even if that voice is . . . voiceless! (Or what we might generously call *technical, impenetrable, chilly,* even *mysterious* as in, "I have no idea what you're writing about.") Then I elaborate on that specific adjective by comparing it with something familiar that kids can relate to. Staying with voice a bit longer, if you think of writing as always having voice, it makes it easier to name for the writer what kind of mood or attitude you're getting from the piece, and how it affects you as a reader. So even a piece that is overwrought with adjectives or awash in run-on sentences could be called, "Lush, like a rain forest. Plump and portly, like an overstuffed chair." Even a piece that has only one sentence or paragraph standing for a much longer story could be called, "Austere; haikulike; like mist or fog." I told a fourth grader that the two little lines she pushed out during a thirty-minute writing workshop that her poem could be published as "Twitter Haiku." I'm not sure she knew what that was (and I might have made it up!), but she positively beamed when I said that.

In the following sections, I offer examples of ways that I talk about or respond in writing to student writing. These samples are similar to the things I truly say when I talk to people about their writing, but of course, in real life, I try to find language and metaphors appropriate to the individual person, the occasion, and the piece of writing.

Unpacking the Top Five Qualities of Good Writing

Voice

When I was in college, taking creative writing classes with published poets, novelists, and nonfiction writers, every one of my teachers had something to say about the quality of *voice* in writing. Someone called it, poetically, "the soul's language." Ben Yagoda interviewed more than forty fiction, nonfiction writers, and poets, and consulted the best style and grammar manuals for his book *The Sound on the Page*, and determined that there is definitely not one true and definitive definition of voice, but that it might more clearly be labeled *style* because writing, or literacy, is truly *not* the same as talking and should not be confused by writing the word *voice* (2004, xxxi). Once, I saw a rubric with the word *style* as a separate quality from *voice*, and bless your hearts if you understand or can teach any difference between them because I cannot. Some assessment checklists also use the words *tone* and even *mood* interchangeably with *voice*, and as soon as you try to question or uncover precisely which word refers to what aspect of text, you've got a heated debate on your hands and a hauling out of literature and composition guidebooks.

Writing friends have discussed with me what constitutes voice in texts, and while we usually come to some consensus that people who write constantly develop an identifiable sound generated from genre preference, topic choice and language tics (unconscious tendencies and patterns in syntax and word choice), we also agree that individual pieces of writing have different voices, depending on what the genre is, why the text is being written, and who is most likely to read it. Most writing friends I've spoken with guard their understandings of voice because it may well be the thing that separates one writer from another; teach it to just anyone, they might argue, and then conceivably, anyone could become a writer! Perhaps my favorite idea of voice comes from novelist Elizabeth McCracken who said, "A writer's voice lives inside his or her bad habits. . . . The trick is to make them charming bad habits. You have to leave some of them alone—basically, leave enough in, so that, if you're Grace Paley, readers *know* it's Grace Paley" (Yagoda 2004, xxviii). Can you imagine saying to kids that their writing voice is a charming amalgamation of bad habits?

The term *voice* is an abstract one; it alludes to all sorts of stylistic and linguistic features of written text, and many stumble when trying to pinpoint precisely what is meant by it. And yet, voice has become the critical feature on many district and state writing rubrics. Teachers include it in lesson plans for both writing and reading. Quite a few books seek to define it, categorize its features, offer examples and suggestions for teaching it. So we need to try to arrive at some kind of definition so that when we exhort kids to write with more voice, or when we wring our hands over their "bad habits," as Elizabeth McCracken argues is the basis of a writing voice, we can try to help students, who may be floundering at first, to find themselves on the page.

In the end, I come to a definition that will not satisfy all readers and writers, but that provides my barometer, my truest feeling for what voice means: a writer's voice encompasses all aspects of writing—style, tone, imagery, structure, choice of words, and even the sound that is built with punctuation—all of which point the way to the heart and soul of what a writer wants to express during the course of a particular piece of writing. Again, what helps me teach kids about voice in texts is to find a juicy adjective for what *kind* of voice it is. So when reading a text like writers, we might say, this voice is playful, honest, risky, observant, a storyteller's voice, a football coach's voice, a drill sergeant's voice, a legal memo voice, a salesperson's voice. Recall from Chapter 3 how groups of teachers named the voice of the narrator in *The Brief Wondrous Life of Oscar Wao* by Junot Díaz, using adjectives like *irreverent*, *sarcastic*, and *clever*. I look for similar adjectives to name and define students' writing voices as I talk with them or write to them about their texts.

> Voice points the way to the heart and soul of what a writer wants to express.

When Jenifer Jeffries and Jennifer Logan, literacy coaches at PS 172 in Brooklyn, New York, and I looked at writing by kindergartners and first graders, we were struck by how the size and shape of letters, how much of the page kids cover with pictures, letters or other marks, and even what colors kids use for print and drawings pointed to a kind of writing voice. After reading through five-year-old Elizabeth's whole writing portfolio, Jennifer let out a big sigh and said, "This little girl is so happy." Jen and I were intrigued, what did she mean? "I'm not sure, but just all the bright color, the mom who appears in every single story and song, the stars, hearts, and flowers that decorate every piece, it's all so bold and joyful."

Jose, a fifth grader in New York City, writes constantly about football, and his sentences fairly bark out information; they are short and choppy and cause his teacher no end of frustration. To me, Jose has a sports broadcaster's voice; I could imagine him barking out his pieces over the noise of a baseball game at Shea Stadium.

At the glorious PS 199 in Queens, New York, I was invited to bring this topic of noticing, naming, and then teaching from the strength and beauty we could find in students' writing to a powerful group of teachers, literacy coach, Mary Dentrone, and Anthony Inzerillo, the kind of visionary, attentive principal every teacher wishes he or she could work with. In an introductory meeting, we studied writing samples that teachers brought with them, and then we went *en masse* into a few classrooms to practice conferring with our newfound language. Anthony moves mountains (or I guess skyscrapers would be a more appropriate analogy for New York City) to clear his schedule so that he can join in when professional developers come to his building, and he actively participates, actively *learns*, alongside the teachers. In a third-grade classroom that day, I asked teachers to pair up and practice conferring with kids, so of course, Anthony had to practice as well. After listening to and peeking at what one boy wrote in his "all about" piece about baseball, Anthony said, "Jerome, your writing voice is so confident; you sound like a 'pro' sports writer! Is there another place in this piece that you could put that 'pro' voice in to teach readers about baseball?" As Anthony walked away from the conference, Mary, his conferring partner, noticed that Jerome actually "grew" in his seat, and she watched him turn to the boys near him, point to his paper, and say, "See, in this place I write like a 'pro'!" Imagine what that boy learned in those five minutes and can carry with him forever: that nonfiction needs a voice of authority, a "pro" voice; and this encouragement came from his elementary school principal.

In addition to naming what kind of voice I hear in students' writing with a specific adjective, I also follow that with a metaphor, or a concrete image that embodies that adjective. For instance, not only is Rachel's writing voice *impromptu* and *syncopated* but it also sounds as if I'm sitting in the coolest piano bar in New York City, listening to a jazz pianist riff on a melody. (By the way, I drew both the adjectives and the concrete image from real life. Rachel, my former fourth- and fifth-grade student did write like jazz music; she grew up to become a magnificent pianist and singer/songwriter who plays in piano bars and jazz clubs, and I sit in those places to listen to her as often as my travels will allow.)

Different Voice for Different Purposes and Audiences

One more important aspect of voice that I must mention is that different texts demand different kinds of voice, depending on the purpose for the text, who the readers will most likely be, and what general genre or type of text the writer wishes to create. Voice might be authoritative, comedic, genteel, pleading, depending on who and what it's for. A letter begging a lover not to leave would differ in tone, word choice, and evidence for the argument from a letter requesting information about graduate programs in dental hygiene or electrical engineering. So this is another idea to pursue with student writers as they read and write texts for different readers and purposes.

I've asked kids in my own classes to play around with different voices, tones, or *registers*, a sociolinguistics term defining a scale of formality in language use. I had my students draft short letters to younger siblings, best friends, parents, the principal, and the United States president, all requesting the same thing: money, longer lunch periods, more time playing video games, or talking on cell phones. Quickly and easily, my students surmised that a change in tone, word choice, and evidence for their arguments had to change with each kind of audience.

Frequent Writing Leads to a Recognizable Style and Voice

So audience and purpose affect voice in writing, and yet, in seasoned and famous writers' works, one can also detect an impermeable style. People who write constantly develop numerous tics, linguistic patterns, and stylistic features that distinguish them from others. We could remove the authors' names from some texts and within a sentence or two, we might determine a poem by e.e. cummings or Gwendolyn Brooks, a short story by Raymond Carver, an essay by June Jordan, an Op-Ed piece by Maureen Dowd, a novel by Gary Paulsen—their writing voices and styles are that pronounced. In creative writing classes, hearing from your teacher that you are developing a distinctive voice is high praise indeed. It means you have stopped sounding exactly like whichever author is in fashion and managed to find your own sentence structures, topics, language, and life perspectives.

In classrooms with young writers, the trick is to notice and name when students begin to take on the styles and persuasions of their favorite authors, but also to move students to embrace and strengthen their individual writing styles. Frankly, the latter is easy if we learn to name the beauty and brilliance in all students' writing, even though it may look and sound unlike our personal tastes, and even though it may not fit tidily into the boxes that evaluative rubrics allow. In truth, young people have sweet, lively, quirky, silly, and profound ways of saying things on paper, and we have only to jump on that to help them grow from there. One graphic demonstration of personal voice I've tried with students is to say, "This piece could only have been written by you. If your name weren't on this, and I just found it in on the floor after class was over, I would know it's yours because of the strength of your writing style."

Five ideas for naming what kind of voice a student writer might have using adjectives, followed by a metaphor or detailed definition of those adjectives that might help make them more concrete, appear on page 62.

Five Ways to Name and Teach Voice

1. Your writing voice is so comfortable—when I read it, it's as if you're sitting with me at the kitchen table, keeping me company.

2. Your writing voice has a quirky, almost smart-alecky quality to it. You sound like the cool, cynical, smart kid in the class, the one everyone is a little afraid of.

3. Your writing voice races along so fast! I feel as if I'm watching and hearing a great chase scene in a cops-and-robbers kind of movie.

4. Your writing voice has a melancholy feel to it, as if you're sitting in front of a window on a grey, rainy day.

5. Your writing voice reminds me of my favorite teacher, who made history come alive in front of us because she told stories about these odd things, sometimes gross things (!), and compared famous people in the past to famous people now, like: "She was the Paris Hilton of her day."

Organization

Perhaps it's because in my daily life I am fairly disorganized, or possibly the word makes me think of big corporations, but I just don't care for the word, *organization*. There is nothing inherently wrong with the word, and yes, we do need to help kids learn to build a logical flow (a sequence, if you will) of sentences and chunks of text so that they create the desired effect, but it just seems an ugly label for a concept and an action that can truly make or break a piece of writing. When I am reading a great book, poem, or article, and I want to gush about it to Randy or a friend, I rarely declare, "It's sequenced!" Instead, I talk about the way a text is shaped, structured, or built. I talk about the architecture of the text. Indeed, when I'm working on my own piece of writing and I'm trying to shape the text, I often turn to architecture or music to give me ideas for how to put the parts together and make them flow meaningfully.

Structuring texts, in fact, is one part of my writing process that turns my energy up high. When I lock on a shape that my thoughts and meanings can fit into, I actually get goose bumps. The draft of my memoir sat, a lump of inert material, for weeks until I read somewhere about the sonata form in music being about, simply put, starting from home, moving away from it, and then coming back home in the end. I quickly cut and moved parts of my narrative around so that I ended up with three major "movements," the first and third glorified the landscape of New Mexico, the place I feel most at home because of the beauty and safety it offered me when I was a little girl.

Many genre forms dictate particular shapes and structures. Stories tend to build tension toward desire and then release from that desire, whether its object was ever attained. Poems tend to use stanzas, line breaks, white space, and distinct or repetitive rhythms to distinguish them from prose. The subjects of feature articles frequently fall into large categories, with perhaps minor clusters of ideas inside those. Academic textbooks famously divide into chapters with headings and subheadings; this very book would fit into that definition.

The problem occurs, I think, when teachers get locked into a short list of rules for how text genres are organized, whereas the world of contemporary literature blows most of those notions apart. We forget that structure should serve meaning, purpose, and art and not the other way around. With strict rules in our heads, we might miss that a story beginning with what happened in the end can actually be a profound and interesting way to tell that specific story. Years ago, I saw a film called *Betrayal*, based on the play by Harold Pinter, about an adulterous affair. The film begins at the very nasty breakup of the affair and travels backward in time through critical scenes revealing the rifts and fights, the betrayals and discoveries that ultimately led to that breakup. The final scene in the movie occurs at the party at which the two lovers meet each other, and in the last second of the film, the camera freezes on an image of the hands of the two lovers touching fingers for the first time. That image of the fingers reaching out transfixed me; it still does in my memory, twenty-six years later. I thought it was so chilling and brilliant, and I wrote in my writer's notebook that night: "Story idea: Can I write something that would tell two connected stories, maybe two points of view, that somehow end in the middle, with the stories going out from there to the beginning and end in time?"

Then I drew two triangles on their sides, their points touching in the middle, with a circle around them, like a bowtie.

One summer I asked my writing institute participants to listen to the keynote speeches with different lenses: one morning for voice, another for word choice, another for organization, and so on. Then during our class, I asked people to find names for those qualities, and I challenged them to move away from rubric language and try to *talk long* about what they noticed. The teachers' responses were extraordinary; I was the lucky recipient of their insights about the voice in my own keynote, and I wish each speaker could have heard what they said each day. When Lester Laminack spoke, we focused on how he organized or structured his speech. The following are how people described Lester's structures. Note that several of them needed graphic depictions, and I highly recommend making little diagrams and sketches to portray different structural elements in writing when you're teaching about it to kids.

1. 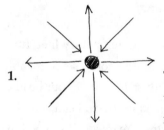 There was a main point in the center of the speech and then all these stories and points went in and out of the main point.

2. Mary Oliver poem with a last line about the sun: → call to action → listing → minispeech → call to action → two stories that connect to teachers → come back to the line about the sun → ask us to reflect on our own lives and then teach differently → back to the poem and the line about the sun.

3. A circle structure. A call to action, with a lot of evidence and examples that would make us want to join in.

4. Personal/Political

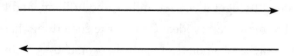

5.

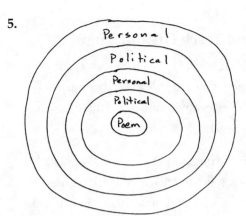

6. Humor

   Passion

   　　Humor

   　　　Passion

7. Like a symphony, with *largo* parts and *staccato* parts.

8. Different modalities: poem, body movements, didacticism. Speech changed course whenever Lester moved from podium to center stage.

The teachers in this course called "Expanding Our Vocabulary for Talking About Student Writing" got excited about talking about structures like writers so that kids can understand and came up with some fantastic ideas: "Reading your piece is like taking a roller-coaster ride, where you're climbing and climbing, anticipating that huge drop; I enjoyed the ride!" Kelle Smith teaches in New Hampshire, and she thought that she could make tangible the concept of a "story mountain" (for the shape of a classic story with rising action, climax, denouement) by naming the actual

Five Ways to Name and Teach Organization

1. The architecture of your piece is so thoughtful of the reader! You used to have a kind of spindly little building that might have toppled over, but now you've made it grand and solid. You've added many floors and put in these elevators (transitions) that help us move more easily.

2. My stomach is dropping in this part of your story! The tension you build is palpable and sensual because you keep holding back from telling us what happened! It's as if by being silent, by not telling us everything, you're making me feel nervous, scared, anxious, even angry for this character.

3. This structure for your memoir is so cool! It's like a scrapbook where each page tells a little story about your trip to Florida: here's the time the alligators almost crawled onto your boat; the time you got sick and your fever was so high, they rubbed ice on your arms and legs; and this page about your brother and his friends jumping off the roof into the swimming pool and you were too afraid to do it so you just held onto the chimney! If it were a scrapbook, you would find little pictures of alligators and ice cubes and a chimney. I can see these pictures inside each of your stories!

4. Reading through the points of your argument in this essay reminds me of looking up at the night sky, where you can see all these clusters of stars, and some of them fall into a design like a constellation that has a name and is a familiar shape to us: Orion's Belt. You've got clusters of ideas and you've gathered them together under different familiar constellations, so I can think about one constellation of ideas before moving on to the next one.

   Or it's like shopping in a toy store. You know how you want to race to your favorite aisle, where the Transformers are or the video games? And you know exactly where to go because the store has arranged the aisles and color-coded them, so you can easily figure out how to get to what you want without wading through stuff you don't want!

5. It's so perfect that your poem has only one stanza! It's as if you want the reader to run headlong through this baseball game you describe to get to the final home run and not pause for any halftime or even a break to buy a hot dog.

local mountain that her students ski on. A New York City teacher thought she could describe the same structure by comparing it not to a mountain but to riding in the subway train and coming out to the giant buildings and flashing lights of Times Square. Another teacher said: "The way you use repetition holds your piece together like the refrain of a song."

Vocabulary or Word Choice

Words are the food and water; the sun, soil, and rain; the fuel and the fortune; the only thing that makes writing, writing. Without words, we would have what—periods, commas, question marks? Words give names to our fury, our thrill, our deepest regret. Words spill out and build up and take us away and let us down and set us straight. Words change minds and hearts. Yet words get little respect when we look at and respond to them in student writing. We tend to notice them only if they're misspelled or lewd, or if they are a bit precocious, more mature or sophisticated than we would expect to come from our nine-, twelve-, and fourteen-year-olds. We skim right over the simple words, like the ones that a boy has chosen to let out, just those for now, about the death of his sweet cat.

In a way, if we paid a heap more attention to the words in our students' writing, we would be teaching them also about voice, structure, even grammar and punctuation! We can teach kids that the words they choose are like big old bullies—they command the reader to look here, pay attention to that, think this, do that. One teacher described a writer's words as "inflammatory," that they made readers get "all riled up." Words are like little pieces of your favorite candy; they pop, they sizzle, they melt in your mouth. We can say to a student, for example, "When I read these words: 'While you are at work every day, your child is changing,' I wanted to go hug my little girl before she grows up and gets away." Or, "When you said, 'Playing this video game puts my mind on pause for awhile,' it made me think that maybe I should buy an Xbox after all! 'Putting your mind on *pause*,' I love that! It sounds like Xbox might help calm me down when I feel stressed."

In traditional language instruction, words have been taught separately from their function inside texts. Most of us received vocabulary lists and were asked to memorize definitions and spellings and use them in sentences. (Someone should publish a book of sentences that generations of kids have plugged their vocabulary words into; they're twisted and stilted and often hysterical!)

Instead, we can and should talk about words in the context of reading published texts constantly. Instead of saying, for instance, that novelist John Banville has a good vocabulary, we can try to be more precise: "Banville dusts off words that have lain unused for a hundred years; Banville's words always mean more than one thing, and you need to pay attention to *all* the meanings." We can notice out loud that the type of words different authors choose depends on the context and the audience for the piece. If this text is a text message asking what corner you're standing on right now so I can find you in the crowd at Times Square, those words will look one way. If this text is the final landmark decision of the Supreme Court that will name the law of the land, those words will take endless hours of debate and testimony, hundreds of drafts and revisions to get exactly right. And when we read students' writing, we can approach their word choices with artists' eyes and marvel about how surprising, fresh, inventive (unheard of?) they can be. Then we can explain what the effects of their words have on us as readers, including the fact that some inventive words may not communicate the student's meaning, or that they might be appropriate inside poems or fiction, but not in an instructional manual for how to fly an airplane.

Five Ways to Name and Teach Vocabulary and Word Choice

1. Your words are so calm and soothing, like a lullaby. They entrance me like a mystical incantation and won't let me go.

2. Your words make me want to get up and dance! They're all bouncy and jivey and sizzling hot.

3. Sometimes you use the most unusual words; they pop right out of the story, like that last popcorn kernel that pops and surprises you as you're opening the bag from the microwave.

4. I love how you use so many exact musical (or science, sports, cooking, dance, art, math, technical) terms for things. You are teaching me, and making me feel smart about learning this new language.

5. Your words are so polite and formal; they remind me of my father, all dressed up in a suit and tie and briefcase, heading off to work at 5:30 every morning.

Sentence Structure and Sentence Fluency

Now sentences, there's a topic I can get passionate about. Sentences are the beautiful bones of writing. Words flesh them out, but the sentence bones build the piece of writing. Those bones are extremely flexible, bendable, breakable, and combinable. Sentences should flow as music flows, but I mean all kinds music, not just "easy listening." Sentences, like music, can be smooth and connected, legato, or choppy and staccato. A writer can only come to this level of music in her sentences from rereading and revision, from looking backward and forward at how one sentence connects to another, and then separating, combining, or completely reimagining them. Unfortunately, the word *fluency* attached to sentence structure confuses the issue. Randy Bomer often notes that fluency in writing is a behavior, not a text feature. Fluency in writing, as it does in reading, describes ease, comfort, perhaps even a certain level of speed, with putting words on paper.

If we take this category to mean variety (rather than comfort and speed) in sentence shapes and structures, then we can talk about how sentences operate in texts. Everyone over the age of forty understands the American cultural jokes about the Dick and Jane reading series popular from the 1930s to the 1970s. Besides the obvious tittering that less mature types let loose around the name "Dick," we can all giggle about the choppy, tedious, leaden meaninglessness of sentences such as "Look Spot. Oh, look. Oh see." Five-year-olds write more complex and meaningful sentences than those.

We can show kids sentences by writers like Virginia Woolf, whose sentences take up an entire page! To understand Woolf, some people parse each sentence, trying to determine the meaning inside every phrase and clause. Other people might say there's nothing but to strap yourself into the rubber raft and ride as if you're on Class IV white water. We could compare Woolf to Gary Paulsen, who is equally famous for his two-word sentences. He uses those (as well as one-sentence paragraphs) to visually and aurally signal distress, tension, or grief. We could demonstrate how sentences operate in a single paragraph, doing the work of moving time forward, of covering vast quantities of information quickly, or of slowing down to paint a richly textured description. Watch the short and long shapes of a few sentences from Walter Dean Myers' memoir, *Bad Boy*, each of which has a job to do.

Harlem is the first place called "home" that I can remember. It was a magical place, alive with music that spilled onto the busy streets from tenement windows and full of colors and smells that filled my senses and made my heart beat faster. The earliest memory I have is of a woman who picked me up on Sunday mornings to take me to Sunday school. She would have five to ten children with her when she rang our bell on 126th Street, and we would go through the streets holding hands and singing "Jesus Loves Me" on our way to Abyssinian Baptist. (2001, 7)

Myers juxtaposes short, informational sentences with longer sentences full of sensual detail, in a kind of back-and-forth, call-and-response rhythm that keeps our attention.

What a different kind of lesson this would be from the infamous sentence diagramming many of us remember from middle school and high school. A sentence in writing is so much more than the sum of its parts, subject and verb.

Five Ways to Name and Teach Sentence Structure

1. These fragments of sentences in the sad part are like little pockets of sorrow. Like teardrops. The fragments stress how isolated you felt.

2. Your sentences race so fast in this part where the character is looking for the murderer. That's exactly how she must be feeling right then, like her heart is racing; she's terrified.

3. These sentences march, steady and straightforward, no questions asked, like they're in the band at a football halftime.

4. You have such a nice variety of sentences, it's like you've cooked up the best soup with long skinny carrots, short stubby potatoes, and a dash of hot pepper (that exclamatory sentence!) to wake up our taste buds.

5. Your sentences all start a different way, some with an introductory word or phrase, some where the subject comes in first, some as a question to the reader; it's as if each one wants to announce itself to the world in a new way.

Details

Probably the most frequent bit of writing advice we give to students is that they need to elaborate. What do we mean? Do we mean to say the text needs to be longer, to have more paragraphs, sentences, words? When the writing task is a prompted essay for test practice (or for the writing test itself), we probably do mean make it longer. But usually, I think that when we are left wanting more from a student text, we might honestly mean that we want to know more; we want to feel something. How often, as a dear friend tells us something that is happening to him, do we say, "Wait, slow down and tell me everything. I want every detail." I think this is a genuinely human trait, that when we are curious and interested in the subject we want surround sound and an IMAX theatre picture. We want *virtual reality*.

Unfortunately, with much student writing, we truly do find that the scene, the argument, or the thought and meaning are thin; we are not drawn into the moment because the moment flashes past, often in bland, emotionless language. So we encourage kids to "add details," and adding details often gets translated into an entreaty to write from the five senses or borrow words from a wall chart called "exciting adjectives." Then our kids' writing is stuffed with sentences that sound silly and empty, or even sound a bit like lies: "My dog." "My brown, cute, long-haired, sad-eyed, short, fat dog." The only place this string of adjectives works is in the song, "The Girl from Ipanema": "Tall and tan and young and lovely. . . ."

Instead, the way to fill out a scene so that it conjures pictures and sounds in readers' minds is to first write honestly and from the heart. When a writer sits squarely inside his or her emotions or recollections of an event and then tells the bitter or embarrassing truth about it, the prose will often contain fewer not more details, shorter not longer sentences, fewer not more adjectives. My friend Dorothy Dickmann, a teacher and a lovely poet, once said, "the human heart has no vocabulary list." When writing truly breaks through to the heart, or when it's about some of the hardest human emotions, often, the simpler, the more profound: "My dad doesn't remember who I am anymore."

A second way to fill out writing is to add layers and texture so that we can see, hear, and feel it. To do this, a writer must relive or reimagine the moment, to climb inside the thing he or she wishes to depict. I often ask kids to pretend they are time traveling to the place, time, and action they are writing about. When they get back

Five Ways to Name and Teach Details

1. This scene has a rough texture; the objects you included—a broken traffic light, a dirty jacket, the pothole in the street, and the cracked sidewalk—all gave me the idea of this being a disheveled neighborhood, a place that no one pays attention to.

2. I must say, when you write about the video game rushing at you from the screen, then yanking to the left and swirling to the right, it almost made me sick to my stomach, but in a good way, like on a roller coaster! Those specific "ing" verbs, present participles, work well in an essay that argues for how kids might learn more if we used thrilling video games to teach boring subjects in school.

3. I would know your grandfather if he walked through our classroom door. You have made your grandfather precisely "Papa" and no other grandfather. His "movie trailer announcer voice," the "sharp shoulder blades poking through his thin shirt," his "gray head, always the tallest in the room," practically make a digital photograph in my mind.

4. You have a way of making the physical surroundings and objects carry so much weight and meaning about your characters and the big ideas of your story. Like how the father has a "Vietnam War medal in a black box that has never been opened," as if he's not proud of it or maybe he's afraid of it? And the teenage boy always accidentally burns things—the toast, the carpet with a candle, even his skin in the summer! It makes me think that his life is in flames, you know? Like it's all going to be consumed and burned to nothing but ashes.

5. Your poem focuses on all the reasons you had to break up with your boy-friend. It's almost like a checklist or a grocery list for readers: "Dear boys, do this, this, this, and this, and believe me, your girlfriend will break up with you!"

from their traveling, I tell them, people will beg for a rich account of the exact sounds, the precise objects, the taste of the strange food, and especially the thought processes and emotions the traveler experienced. "So put on your extrasensory recording devices," I tell kids, "and take us with you to that place and time."

In one of my favorite films, called *Nobody Knows*, Japanese director, Kore-eda, wraps his story around with such layers of detail that you feel you might almost drown in it. This devastatingly sad story involves four young children living alone in their apartment in Tokyo, trying to create lives for themselves after their mother abandons them. Kore-eda places his film camera low, at the height of the children, and points it, sometimes for an uncomfortable amount of time, on objects: shoes, crayons on the floor, hands, a toy piano, and he repeats those images until they become larger-than-life. Kore-eda explained in the interview included on the DVD that these objects are "delicate, tangible, and specific." He said he wanted "these images [to] grow inside you, the minute the movie is over." This was precisely the effect his film had on me, and the image of the littlest girl's shoe haunted me for days. The way to pull readers in is not necessarily to add empty adjectives, but rather to stay with the objects, the nouns, sometimes for a long time, until the images grow inside of the reader.

Language Tools for Reading and Responding to Student Writing

With reading, writing, and practice, we can all increase our "vocabulary" for talking about student writing. We can see that the language of rubrics and standards, while it might have an evaluative function as one kind of measure, limits what we notice and name about the genuine craft our students accomplish in their writing. It would be far better to imitate how writers and artists of all types talk about their work so that we can apply language that is more artful, descriptive, and concrete. By using more elegant and sophisticated language for naming what our students are doing, we can actually teach them what to reach for as they compose and revise, and how to articulate their writing processes. See page 74 for a list of some of the writing qualities I most value when I read published and student-authored texts.

The Characteristics of Good Writing

- Honesty
- Wide-awakeness to the world (noticing what hides in the shadows, caring for the quiet, the vulnerable, and unseen)
- Feeling of discovery and inquiry
- Unusual formulations; "Not the way to say it" (Kundera 2000)
- Brave, fun, out-on-a-limb comparisons
- Clear and personal or original thinking
- Multiple perspectives, empathy for other's life situations and points of view
- Strong sensory images
- Strong evocation of place
- Music in the sentences (prose) or lines (poetry)
- Purposeful repetition
- Sense of storytelling
- Build up of tension
- Developed narrative scenes that conjure up pictures, sounds, and emotions in the reader's mind
- An ear for the way different types of people talk, in different circumstances, and in different roles and social relationships
- Control of time
- Complicated character(s) who are full of contradictions: not all good and not all bad
- Deepening thoughts and ideas by layering with questions, quotes, facts, statistics, and opposing points of view
- Respect for the reader (understands and anticipates readers' questions and needs)
- Window on the writer (values, purposes, intelligence, sense of humor)
- Style (morose, ironic, macho, light, urgent, languorous, elegant, violent, tender)

Where Can We Find Fun Phrases for Talking About Writing?

Often, teachers tell me that they wish to notice and name the gems in student writing and to teach qualities of good writing using the language of the trade, but not being writers themselves, they are not sure how to find words to express what they feel when they read kids' work. How do we know what words to say, what *long language* to use to name the craft in our students' writing? This chapter outlines some of my favorite places to find fun and unusual descriptions of art and craft that help me have a storehouse full of things to say.

New Places to Find Language for Responding to Writing

From Personal Reading of All Kinds of Texts

First, we must read widely—even read things that annoy us or that aren't to our taste because those things can give us new lenses through which to see our students' work. Periodically, I park myself in my local Borders bookstore, order the largest size coffee, and peruse magazines about subjects, like skateboarding, that I don't care much about but that kids care a great deal about.

In Chapter 3, I enumerated the importance and benefits of learning to read like a writer in order to learn from and imitate qualities of strong writing. I provided protocols for how to read published writing, point to places that burst from the page, and describe what the effects are for each reader. Here, I'll make another impassioned plea that we find a home for reading in the daily rush of our busy lives. We know, from endless quotes from writers, that they learned how to write well from reading, often from an early age. So it makes sense that as teachers we would also benefit from turning a writer's eye to the books, magazine articles, sports columns, editorials, blogs, even the ads and instruction manuals we read in the course of living our lives. These texts teach us how words can look and sound on the page, and most often, they can offer up surprising differences from the staid old notions of good writing that we picked up in our own schooling.

As educators in charge of children's literacy learning, we are responsible to study the how-to manuals of our subject; that is, written texts of all kinds. Knowing the rudiments of comma usage and the intricacies of phrases, clauses, and sentence structures, while crucial for building readable and meaningful pieces of writing, does not create good writers. Good writers are those who open their eyes, ears, hearts, and minds to the world and realize that the world gives endlessly and generously to ideas for writing. Good writers realize that they have to write every single day, often for a long stretch of time, and that they will have to revise their work dozens and dozens of times until it begins to approach the vision in their heads. Good writers consider reading a *nonnegotiable* routine in their workdays, and in fact, turn to reading for their writing lessons. Ted Kooser, former United States Poet Laureate and a deeply thoughtful teacher, suggests that to learn how to write a poem, you need to first read 100 poems.

While most of us do not aspire to the tough disciplines of professional writers' lives, if we want to be great writing teachers, we need to make the act of reading like writers more direct, more accessible, a habit we get into no matter how the day goes. I know teachers who dedicate mornings to Bible reading, who read detective novels like eating chocolate, who devour blogs and other online communications, who skim magazine articles as they walk on the treadmill, who relax with a book the last half hour before bed, or who grab a few moments to read while eating their cereal early in the morning. We also need to read widely, casting our eyes over all kinds of texts from persuasive advertising copy to the essayistic tone of blogs to the short, pithy turns of phrase in Twitter tweets. The point is to read so that we can teach with insider knowledge our lessons about both reading and writing.

Reading Clubs

A sure way to develop a strong reading life and have fun and get support while doing it is to join (or form your own) a reading club that meets to discuss literature. When you make a commitment to meet at a certain place and time each month, you are more likely to get the agreed-upon reading done, even if you have to cram it in the night before. You will have friends to help you work through the hard parts, and you'll dive into texts that you might not have chosen on your own. You'll expand your universe through the words and ideas of different authors, different cultures and countries, and different eras.

You might prefer to sponsor a reading club in your school, so that you can be sure to get to it before you leave the building and enter that zombie state of exhaustion the second you put your bags down at home and head for the couch/bed/TV/computer. Or you might enjoy an off-campus book club in the luxury of people's homes, with the possibilities of serious food and wine—either way, book clubs can be places to make friends and feed yourselves emotionally and intellectually. Most book clubs I've belonged to have made it part of our challenge to read texts we know we wouldn't attempt on our own: the classics we missed in college, the latest Man Booker Prize winner, or a collection of poems, so this might be an opportunity for you as well to keep up with the diversity of texts available to readers.

From Personal Writing of All Kinds of Texts

Ever since Lucy Calkins hired me to be a professional developer at the Teachers College Reading and Writing Project over twenty years ago, I have thought it my job to invite, seduce, even beg teachers to join in the pleasures and benefits of doing their own writing in order to expand their knowledge of and vocabulary for teaching writing to their students. Teaching writing without doing it ourselves is like trying to teach a four-year-old how to tie shoes when we have only worn flip-flops our entire life. We may have learned some language to use or even a little sing-songy rhyme: *up and over, around and through, this is how to tie your shoe!* But the direct experience of a process is not there; the confidence that solutions can be found and that things will come out all right in the end is not there. Once I was swimming in a calm little bay of Abiquiu Lake in New Mexico, and I watched as a grandmother was teaching her four-year-old granddaughter to swim. She held one hand lightly beneath the little girl's tummy and enthusiastically invited her to "Kick! Kick! Kick!" The little girl's mother stood on the beach, refusing her daughter's imploring voice to come join them in the water. "I can't swim!" the mother whined, looking frightened.

The grandmother said, "When your mama was little, I used to put her on my back and swim all the way across this bay."

Suddenly, her grown daughter's face lit up and she shouted, "I remember that!" And though she was all gussied up, wearing jewelry, with her hair nicely blow-dried, she began to roll her pants up and wade deeper in, saying that suddenly, she wanted to swim too. It seemed that reminding her of that direct experience of doing it, of physically moving through the water, triggered her confidence that indeed, she *did* know how to swim.

Getting any writing done, while also teaching, raising families, pursuing sports and other passions, is very difficult, as I know all too well. So, as with the suggestions for reading more, we have to find times, places, and support systems for doing our own writing. My first bit of advice is to seek out a continuing education class at a local college or university. A class provides both writing instruction from someone who is likely to be a practicing, published writer, and also an audience and peer support from other class members. You can also find writing teachers and classes online, and while they lack the joys of face-to-face contact, they still provide audience and response.

Writing Clubs

You might decide to join or form your own in-school writing club, similar to a book club, but its members write and respond to each other's writing instead of other authors' writing. When I taught at PS 11 in Chelsea, New York City, my first principal, Leslie Gordon, a few teachers, and even our math consultant, who joined us whenever she was in town from California, met at 7 o'clock in the morning to talk about our writing. I was working on a young adult novel, and my friends' advice to get to some action right away and drop so much internal thinking and lyrical description was spot-on for my intended audience of preteens.

The prospect of having a writing club that meets in people's homes, as with book clubs, offers time and an environment to relax and let loose in ways that are untenable in school settings. Barbara Clements, Fran McCraken, and Mary Samuels began a writing club when I worked in their elementary school in Washington, DC. They meet in homes and in quiet restaurants, where they can enjoy dinner as well as discussion. The group has continued to meet for several years, and their writing has evolved so much with each other's support that they are now looking toward publishing some of their work.

Listening to Artists, Musicians, Architects, Choreographers, Filmmakers, Chefs, and Fashion Designers Talk About Their Art and Craft

The most instructive thing for my writing knowledge and craft is having conversations with other writers, or watching and listening to artists and craftpersons of all kinds at work. Listening to directors and actors in the special feature commentary on film DVDs, or watching those interior design shows like *Design on a Dime* can give me new words to describe how to structure a poem or narrative or how to use color and light to create mood in writing. We can all borrow from a maker of anything who articulates his or her process for us. The only challenge is to remember what they said! Here are some recent examples from my daily reading, viewing, eavesdropping, and unscientific research sampling of various artists and craftspersons that I was able to scribble into my writer's notebook:

- Gracie, my hair stylist (and colorist), said that she gets ideas for hair and makeup design from places as divergent as party designs, wedding cakes, and nature. She chose for my hair color a shade that looks, "More like sunlight than sand," she said; and I said, "Yeah! You rock, girl! Make me look like sunlight!"
- In a skateboarding magazine called *Concrete Wave* (cool title!), I found a fascinating article called "Defamiliarization," where author Marcus Bandy claims that skateboarders are artists because they transform ordinary objects (a drainage ditch, a brick embankment, a marble bench, even a handrail) into surfaces to skate on. "Skateboarding challenges perception; perception is made difficult and form is challenged. A handrail is no longer just a handrail, but is also a prop, a tool, an obstacle—an art supply" (2009, 58).
- Clive James, my favorite literary and cultural critic, might argue some with my premise in Chapter 3 that writers learn from reading. He says, "Writers tend to

think the way they write was influenced by literature . . . but a writer's ideal of a properly built sentence might just as well have been formed when he was still in short pants and watched someone make an unusually neat sandcastle" (2007, 28). James goes on: "I learned a lot about writing from watching an older friend sanding down the freshly dried paint on his rebuilt motorbike so that he could give it another coat: he was after deep rich, pure glow" (29). Wow! Sanding down what you already painted: this is an excellent metaphor to share with kids about what and why to revise. They might rather sand a motorbike, but still. And finally, James says, "For the way I thought prose should move I learned a lot from jazz. From the moment I learned to hear them in music, syncopation and rhythm were what I wanted to get into my writing" (29).

- In her book called *Gardening at the Dragon's Gate*, Wendy Johnson says that to garden is to look at "every leaf, every big-eyed bug, every rusty wheelbarrow [as] both familiar and strangely new at the same time" (2008, xii). Surely she is speaking about the *act of writing* as well as the act of turning soil, planting seeds, watering, and harvesting!

- One of my best friends from high school, Larry Deemer, is an artist. Recently, one of his paintings was chosen for a gallery showing in New York City, conveniently while I was in town, and we went to the gallery together. His piece, called *oh baby*, was small, a twelve-by-twelve-inch square, that depicted only a rosy, O-shaped mouth, plus the chin, and upper-right chest and part of the arm of a baby. Larry described to me what he had in mind as he created this piece: "I was trying to see how *little* of the body I could put in the frame that would still communicate *baby-ness*. It's a classical subject but I was kind of making it into an abstraction, I think."

  As it turns out, it took very little of the body to signal *baby*. Larry captured something about the subtle hues and tones of the flesh, the plumpness of it, and the sweet rosy mouth that shouted, "I am a baby!"

  Wow, I thought. That's an interesting exercise. I try to accomplish something like that in my poems all the time. My favorite (though often painful) revision strategy is to cut to the fewest words to carry the greatest meaning. I could imagine saying to a young writer, who has just the bare minimum of sentences about a character or setting or emotion: "You figured out how to communicate your meaning, the manga-ness of Japanese manga, the skateboard-ness of skateboarding, in just these few, spare words. But I knew instantly that that's what you meant because you chose the perfect words to stand for that big idea!"

- Any kind of talking or writing about art can yield useful and lovely language for naming the visual qualities, the imagery and descriptions that we're always imploring our students to master in their writing. In a book called *50 Artists You Should Know*, the author, Thomas Köster, describes Caravaggio's oils in a way that makes me feel as if I can touch the paintings. "His still lifes show even the worm-holes in the apple and the discoloration of the leaves, and in his pictures of saints even the dirty soles of the praying figure's feet can be made out" (2006, 51). And here is a quote from Picasso talking about the dreamlike quality of Marc Chagall's paintings: "When Chagall paints, one does not know whether he happens to be asleep or awake. He must have an angel somewhere in his head" (133).

- Hirokazu Kore-eda, my favorite Japanese filmmaker, talks in the director's commentary segment included on the DVD, about his stunningly beautiful film *Maborosi* like this: "I wanted to show a contrast between this scene—open, with lots of movement—and the scenes back in Osaka—which are close in space, with a claustrophobic feeling. I wanted to show the twin themes of loss and memory." Look at that new, concrete language we could use with a student writer: "I notice you often write about the twin themes of loss and memory." Or, "I notice a contrast between an open space full of movement out on the football field and this closed claustrophobic space in the classroom."

- In the commentary section on the DVD of the Disney animated film, *Ratatouille*, there is a brilliant clip that aligns the creative processes of Brad Bird, the film's artist, animator, writer, and director, with that of the famed chef Thomas Keller, who lent his artistry and technical knowledge to the little mouse who cooks. Both men had mentors and role models in their pursuit of artistic greatness. Both describe a sense of urgency in the moment of creation, an emotional attachment to the project, and a desire to create something that will please their audience. Chef Keller mentions feeling proud to present a beautiful dish and feeling extreme pleasure when his "audience" loved their food.

The best tips for sharing with our student writers is that both artists spoke of letting go of control of the process, of pushing themselves to greatness, to making the one film shot or ratatouille dish that no one else has made, "tweaking it left of center," says Chef Keller. He also maintains that when he mentors young chefs, he does not criticize them because that shuts them down; rather, he lets them try something, and own it (both successes and failures), and that raises their desire to keep trying. Wise words for teaching writing, and they come from a person who cooks for a living.

Reviews and Literary Criticism

Listen to how Margaret Wise Brown's biographer, Leonard Marcus, talks about reading *Goodnight Moon* for the very first time as an adult:

> I was forcibly struck by the realization that the quietly compelling words I was saying over in my head were poetry and, what was more, poetry of a kind I prized: accessible but not predictable, emotional but purged of sentiment, vivid but so spare that every word felt necessary. Her words seemed to be rooted in the concrete but touched by an appreciation of the elusive, the paradoxical, the mysterious.
>
> There was astonishing tenderness and authority in the voice, and something mythic in it as well. It was as though the author had just now seen the world for the first time, and had chosen to honor it by taking its true measure in words. (1992, 3)

Goodnight Moon is one of my top ten favorite children's books in all the world, and I agree with his assessment of the mysterious and emotional, yet unsentimental poetry of it; but *mythic*, I'm not sure. Marcus clearly loves the subject of his biography, as a good biographer should, but his language for this simple, forty-eight-word picture book might be a tad bit over the top. Imagine though, that you were Margaret Wise Brown and could have these words written about your work? Better yet, imagine saying to a sixth grader that his words are *the kind of poetry you prize*, or that he has written as if he has *just now seen the world for the first time and has honored it with his words*. That would make him want to keep writing, I guarantee it.

Just for fun, and for an extreme contrast in how the language of response can look and sound, let's apply this standard example, available to anyone who searches for "writing rubric" online, to *Goodnight Moon:*

Qualitative Features of Writing Checklist

Communication

_____ Story communicates thoughts and ideas.

_____ Story has a logical organizational structure or sequence.

_____ Story has effective strategies for organizing information.

_____ Story has sentence-to-sentence and word-to-word relationships.

Hmmm . . . I *guess* the story communicates thoughts and ideas; I suppose the structure is logical enough. *Probably* Ms. Brown had some good strategies for sequencing all the objects to say goodnight to, but I wouldn't say she has organized her information (why is that item repeated on the same checklist anyway?).

At any rate, there is no room on this checklist to account for the magical, transfixing nature of this text for generations of babies and toddlers. There is no room to celebrate her delightful inclusion of the phrase "goodnight mush" to rhyme with "quiet old lady whispering hush." There is not a line item on the checklist that can account for the fact that Clement Hurd's heartbreakingly sweet illustrations depict character qualities (they are bunnies, not humans), actions, and meanings, as well as a sense of deep tenderness that is not necessarily communicated in the words.

The best place to find language that would most capture the attention of your students is from movie and video game reviews. These are the worlds our kids thrill to and thrive in, and rather than decry their existence, we should steal their language for our own purposes. Listen to the lively language in this review of *Dark Night*, the Batman movie, directed by Christopher Nolan: "At two hours and 32 minutes, this is almost too much movie, but it has a malicious, careening zest all its own. It's a ride for the gut *and* the brain" (Gleiberman 2008). *Malicious* and *careening zest*—try using those words next time you confer with a student whose entire essay is only two paragraphs!

Julieanne Harnatz, who teaches in San Pedro, California, had the most perfect idea while we talked about learning how to name student writing from reading book reviews. She said, "I could take a book reviewer's stance. I could walk around the room during writing conferences thinking 'If I were going to write a book review of your writing, what would I write?'" If we all did that, we could completely change the discourse for how teachers comment on student writing.

Blurbs on the Backs of Books

One of my favorite places to learn new language for responding to writing is from blurbs on the backs of books. Blurbs are a subgenre unto themselves, often written by famous writers so they're bound to be well crafted. Since the purpose of the blurbs is to sell books, they are going to sound effusive and sometimes offer rather empty praise: Glorious! Superb! Fantastic! But study the longer blurbs from the backs of a few books and you'll find a rich list of phrases to borrow.

Here are a few examples from random books from our bookshelves:

Being a Black Man: At the Corner of Progress and Peril, edited by Kevin Merida: "Written with clarity and painstaking candor, [this book] takes you on a journey of potential and promise, pitfalls and peril. It will have you laughing, crying, shouting, and praying for an answer to the twenty-first-century's greatest dilemma—the challenge of creating a path for young black boys to become successful men."

—Charles J. Ogletree Jr.

The Graveyard by Neil Gaiman: " . . . a novel that showcases [Gaiman's] effortless feel for narrative, his flawless instincts for suspense, and above all, his dark, almost silky sense of humor."

—Joe Hill

War and Peace by Leo Tolstoy: "The book is 'about everything that counts.'"

—Simon Schama

Designs on the Heart: The Homemade Art of Grandma Moses by Karal Ann Marling: "In Grandma's [Moses'] pictures, you could go home again even if you had never seen a farm before."

The Sea by John Banville: "A brilliant, sensuous, discombobulating novel."

—The Spectator

Say You Are One of Them by Uwem Akpan: ". . . is a beautiful, bitter, compelling read. The savagely strange juxtapositions in these stories are grounded by the loving relationships between brothers and sisters forced to survive in a world of dreamlike horror. Open the book at any page, as in divination, and a stunning sentence will leap out."

—*Louise Erdrich*

I, for one, intend to use one day soon Joe Hill's comment about Neil Gaiman's "dark, almost *silky* sense of humor" to name what a young person does well. Or "discombobulating"—I'm going to try that on some unsuspecting student! The trick is to take some of this high-falutin' writerly language from book blurbs and use it in place of the clunky, business-sounding words we often apply to writing in classrooms. Instead of "It's sequenced," how about, "Your story unfolds like a bolt of fine silk, delicately, quickly, smoothly." Rather than "good vocabulary," how about, "You use such joyful and jaunty words despite living in such a difficult situation; it's as if you're really trying to make this tragic story more palatable for your reader."

One summer, I took my Teachers College Writing Institute classes to the Columbia University bookstore on a field trip. I invited teachers to spread out all over the store, especially to sections they might not usually spend time in—sports, technology manuals, music, and architecture, to spy on the book blurbs for new precision language for complimenting writing. I'm sure the bookstore clerks thought the store was being invaded by geeks, when all over the floor we could hear "Read this!" or "Here's a great one!" The teachers were so excited; they came rushing to me with examples they found on the backs of cookbooks, parenting guides, even inspirational quotes on magnets and bookmarks on a rack near the checkout counter. Andrea Smith, one of the teachers, shared her insight that she feels teachers have been conditioned to think in "education terminology." She found beautiful quotes on the backs of self-help books that she said, "actually could help us reconnect to the purpose of why we write."

When we got back to our classroom, teachers shared the phrases from backs of books they found on our scavenger hunt. The group of primary teachers were geniuses at translating the effusive, overblown language meant to sell adult books into "kid-friendly" language:

just plain fun

a generous gift for anyone who reads it

makes me want to pack my suitcase and go to this place!

characters who feel like they could be your best friends

swings from funny to sad

comes as a bolt from the blue

crackles and pops

a story as comfortable as an old pair of jeans

a hair-raising story

deliciously funny

a classic in the making

smart and sassy

breathes new life into a familiar story

makes you want to grab the person next to you and say, "Read this!"

unputdownable

impossible to read without falling in love

it's like dessert at the end of a meal

[the author] listened to what her heart might say

as sweet and nourishing as fresh summer corn

so clear, like X-ray vision

the voice is a clear trumpet in the midst of noise

words that dance, weep, fight, love, and perform miracles

Zen-like simplicity

it reads like a ride in a car without brakes

a love letter to basketball

That last one is my favorite, and I've used it several times when I face yet another blow-by-blow description of a football or soccer game. I witnessed it myself: those words work. The writers of these "love-letters" to their beloved sport of _____ (fill in any kind) couldn't wait to write more!

Develop Language in Collaboration with Your Students

Last, but most important, we can find the way to name aspects of writing that connect with students' lives and interests by asking *them* what to call things. Kids have surprisingly analytical gifts for digging into texts and naming what they notice and admire there. What they may not have is the official literary term for things. Not yet, anyway. I want them to first talk long about the techniques they notice writers using, just as I talk long when I'm naming what I notice student writers doing.

After we make kids' noticing of writing tools and techniques public on a chart, a PowerPoint presentation, or on handouts in kids' writing folders, I can add in the literary or grammatical term: *complex sentence; first, second, third person; stanza; white space*; or whatever the term might be. As Katie Wood Ray notes, having names for writing craft that are devised by the classroom community makes it easier for you and your students to talk about what you're thinking and doing as you compose and respond. She writes, "You'll want to choose a name for the technique that captures the essence of how that technique is used. The names are often short phrases, and you need not put pressure on yourself to make them cute or clever" (1999, 124). Ray also notes that craft names can and will get shortened to nicknames if you and your kids use them often. For example, recall the story I told about the sixth grader in Kate Kuonen's classroom in Indianapolis in Chapter 3, who described metaphor as a "disguise" for something else.

Noticing Craft in What Students Do and Make in the Course of a Day

Writing is only one of thousands of things students are learning how to do in school. If we connect writing to other content areas, we can tap into kids' passions and talents that may not present themselves as kids write. We're often pleasantly surprised when a student makes a connection between the structures and features of the mystery novel he is reading energetically and the short fiction story that he is writing, or when a science or social studies topic becomes the source of a nonfiction feature article. We can make it our goal to sponsor learning connections across the day by repeating structures, concepts, and language of our teaching. Becoming aware and attuned to students making the connections for themselves requires the same kind of *noticing* and *naming* that I wrote about in the preceding chapters. When we name for kids the similarities between revising thinking while solving math problems and revising writing, or observing the world for sensory details to add into writing drafts, or observing closely and taking detailed notes on the science experiment, we have helped our students fuse their learning connections and strengthen critical concepts. We can literally see the *ahas* light up kids' faces.

Often educators talk about teaching the whole child, but when we read student work, we treat kids as if all there is in the world is writing workshop and pieces of paper with marks on them. Even secondary teachers must teach the whole child, as least as best we can, given the sliced-and-diced nature of our school days. We remind kids of their strengths in this or that subject; we compare the strategies necessary in one discipline area to those of another; we admire the gifts and intelligences individuals bring to our learning communities.

Unfortunately, as upper-grade and secondary literacy teachers, we have to work even harder to learn what our kids know and can do in places outside our immediate classroom environment. In many schools, fourth and fifth grades imitate secondary schools, with kids going to different teachers for literacy, math, science, and social studies. It becomes difficult not to put kids into little compartments when we see them only through the lens of literacy competencies, and we are largely unaware of their intelligences of observation, building, movement, knowledge of the natural world, numeracy, music, and art. If a student

> If students flounder in reading, or . . . hate writing, we only see them forever floundering and hating.

flounders in reading, or visibly and verbally hates writing, we only see them forever floundering and hating. We lose sight of the child who comes alive in the science lab or on the track outside.

As often as possible, then, we can try to smooth the edges between literacy learning and other disciplines in our students' school days. Teachers can notice kids in other settings and use the specificity of that: how they observed that plant growing; how they decided to use a half nelson pin instead of a full nelson during the wrestling match; how they solved that math problem "simply but elegantly" and can use that language to apply to learning about craft in writing. I once made a huge breakthrough with a fifth-grade boy in my class who was less than thrilled about developing his writing beyond short, terse sentences, by spying on him during gym class. He was a truly gifted soccer player, and watching him float around the soccer field, almost tapping the ball but sending it skillfully between the legs of his poor rival team, gave me the language to use in a writing conference. I asked him how he did that, how he seemed to barely touch the ball and yet make it travel so far across the field, and he said he knew how to find the ball's "sweet spot."

"Oh, it's the same in writing!" I said. "I try to find just the right image, the sweet spot, to describe something for my reader." On one hand, the soccer example helped me know what to say in that one conference. On the other hand, it also taught the writer that writing draws on all his talents and intelligences, things he knows from many domains.

Now that we are equipped with this array of resources for looking at all student writing to notice and name the gems we find, let's practice doing so in the next two chapters with a number of samples of student writing that I've collected from my own and other classrooms around the country.

6
How Can We Read Student Writing to Find the Hidden Gems?

For I will consider my Cat Jeoffry . . .

For when he takes his prey he plays with it to give it a chance . . .

For one mouse in seven escapes by his dallying . . .

For in his morning orisons he loves the sun and the sun loves him

For he has the subtlety and hissing of a serpent, which in goodness he suppresses . . . .

For he will not do destruction if he is well-fed, neither will he spit without provocation . . . .

For he is the quickest to his mark of any creature . . .

For there is nothing sweeter than his peace when at rest . . .

For there is nothing brisker than his life when in motion . . .

For his tongue is exceeding pure so that it has in purity what it wants in music . . .

For by stroking him I have found out electricity . . .

—CHRISTOPHER SMART, from "Jubliate Agno"

Christopher Smart, an eighteenth-century English poet, devoted a small portion of his religious paean to God, "Jubliate Agno" (written while he was incarcerated in a "madhouse"), to this homage to his cat, whom he considered the most perfect of God's creatures. Smart watched Jeoffry so intently, scrutinizing the cat's every waking and sleeping motion. He exalted over every miniscule detail of Jeoffry's body and activity, from the most obvious feature of Jeoffry's cat-ness: "he goes in quest for food"; to the most superlative, "For his motions on the earth are more than any other quadruped." To Smart's loving, observing, poetic eye, Jeoffry became unmatched, an übercat. That lucky duck-cat had in his owner, Christopher Smart, the most captive and appreciative audience ever known to cat-kind. What if we knew our students' writing so intensely? What if we glorified the most mundane aspect of their work in the soaring language of a poet?

In their book, *Persons in Process*, Anne Herrington and Marcia Curtis research the unbelievably moving stories of four college students who struggle with serious personal and life issues, and who have also borne almost two decades of failures, for a variety of reasons, in their attempts to communicate in writing. Herrington and Curtis read their writing with the most respectful, generous eyes, and by doing so they embody powerful roles as audience for their students' writing and becoming. They write, "By presenting ourselves to students as . . . an audience able to comprehend their writing we help them express themselves more coherently, both over time and in the present moments of their writing for us" (2000, 205). Their research reveals plenty of evidence of the opposite, when teacher response has been "downright hostile" resulting in "nearly incoherent prose." They claim that teachers must approach student writing as an act of faith, participating in what Peter Elbow calls the "believing game" or Coleridge calls a "willing suspension of disbelief." "It is an act both of human and of poetic faith allowing us to hear the writer's voice within our students' work even before it has been given full throat. And the simple matter is, if we refuse to hear it, we constrict it; if, bent on playing instead 'the doubting game,' we refuse to nurture it as it comes to us, we cannot be part of calling it forth" (206).

I have witnessed groups of caring teachers read student writing, calling forth student voices even from texts that have not yet given "full throat." A group of secondary teachers, literacy coaches, principals, and vice principals sat with me around a table one morning, two weeks into the new school year in Sunnyside, Washington, reading their students' first writing samples of the year while following the protocol for reading student writing I outline in Appendix A. Some began to whisper to the person next to them, "You gotta hear this one!" Appreciative giggles for kids' quirky ways with words bubbled up around the table. Suddenly, my friend and colleague, Gaby Layden, said, "Excuse me—can I just read this beginning to everyone?" We oohed and ahhed over eighth grader Yesenia's first sentences. Someone else read an ending, and then others jumped in to share bits and pieces from the samples they were reading. Then several of us nudged Karen Walker, a sixth-grade teacher, to read aloud a clever condemnation of the writing process by one of her kids, and several of us asked for copies of that piece.

Karen was hesitant to read another of her students' personal narratives out loud, but we insisted, and she did a fine job with this repugnant, but hysterical rendering of the time the author and his friends found a "turd" in the family toilet bowl. We all gagged and yelled, "Yuck!" and added our own funny turns of phrase, as people do when stories tickle them. We all grew silent and weepy over several honest pieces about kids living with gang violence, family members in jail, and other kinds of chaos that we could not possibly imagine.

At one point, I interrupted to say, "I wish we had videotaped this sharing session. The kids who wrote these pieces should be able to watch a group of adults, particularly their teachers and principals, whooping and hollering and weeping over their writing. We could create whole classrooms of future writers, just by letting them see and hear our responses." (I still think, after witnessing many groups of teachers all over the country reacting with genuine glee and sorrow over student writing that someone should follow up on my suggestion and let me know what happens when the kids watch the film.)

I think what helps groups of teachers enjoy themselves while reading their kids' writing is that I invite them to read, for ten full minutes, with eyes for the beauty and brilliance that exists in every piece. I ask teachers to relax and know that we will have plenty of time across the year to address student needs. *Relax?* How often can teachers do that? We're so pressed to teach, correct, teach, correct that we often pass over what *is* there, in our rush to find what *isn't* there.

> We often pass over what *is* there, in our rush to find what *isn't* there.

Usually, when we read texts for our own pleasure or education, we read in a relaxed manner, and we read for humor, beauty, brilliance, and information. We read to find ourselves in characters' stories, to relate to life circumstances, to be stirred emotionally, to escape our worries, and to expand our worlds. When most of us approach a published text—whether a novel from the best-seller list or a form we have to fill out for medical insurance—we read with an attitude of respect. Even if we don't like it, if a text is printed on official-looking paper, or between cardboard covers, or posted on an accredited website, and especially if the author is critically acclaimed, we assume the writer knows what he or she is doing, and we allow a whole lot of leeway in style as well as substance. We assume the sentences make sense, and that our job as readers is to figure it out. We have more or less success, depending on the type of text and how much it simplifies or explains for its audience. Whatever we don't understand, whatever questions we are left with or confusions we feel, we automatically attribute to a personal lack of intelligence or reading skill.

If we love the text we're reading, we become transfixed; we continue to turn pages well into the night, disrupt our routines to keep going, underline places that are beautiful or that speak to our beliefs, values, and yearnings. We might even read bits out loud to ourselves (no, we're not crazy, we just want that memorable language to ring in our ears). We reread (sometimes more than once) when we lose our place, and occasionally look up words and facts on the Internet. We carry our reading in our heads after we've closed the book, while we're dicing vegetables for dinner, or showering, or driving. When events, places, or objects in life occur that relate to things in our books, we feel excited—we say to anyone who will listen: "I just read about this place in my book!" We recall phrases of text or lines of poems and songs and use the language of writers to narrate our experiences in the world around us like "All the world's a stage, and all the men and women merely players" (*As You Like It*, Shakespeare) or "Star light, star bright, first star I see tonight."

We try to find others who will talk with us about what we read. We can hardly contain ourselves: "*In this great book I'm reading. . . .*" We seek friends or book clubs with whom we can experience the joy of sharing a text and discussing it. We look forward to what Betsy has to say about the mother in this book, or to what Ed has to say about how men are always portrayed, often in such stereotypical, unsubtle ways. And mostly, we anticipate the new insights, explanations, and life experiences others in the group bring to this text. Our eyes open, our horizons expand, our perspectives change and grow from the meaning that others make.

How stunning it would be if we could all read our students' texts with this same respect and anticipation! We would certainly enjoy doing it more, and the gifts of honest human response we would bring to our students could last them a lifetime of writing. Instead, we read with *dread*, anticipating the worst from struggling writers, sighing with dismay that so-and-so *still* hasn't learned how to paragraph, even though we've drilled them on that topic all year long. We read with rubrics and grades in our minds, hating this kind of evaluation, and harboring misgivings that our judgments can only be subjective, that we can't possibly know what grade to assign any bit of writing that slips beneath the obvious A or so-called exemplary papers.

We analyze student writing for its organization (or lack thereof), vocabulary, sentence variety, and T-units, to determine what level it's on. Sometimes, we decide that many of our children have "no language" for writing because they don't choose the kinds of words ("sparkle" words, according to one test prep package) that have been granted status and value by writing programs and standardized writing test rubrics. And that's not fair. I promise you that we could submit some famous contemporary prose and poetry to the same measures, and they would come in at a very low level indeed!

So why is it so hard to think of student writing as art and to presume intention, skill, and talent on the part of our children?

You probably know the book *The Dot*, by Peter Reynolds, about a little girl named Vashti, who has only a blank piece of paper at the end of art class and refuses to try to paint. Her art teacher suggests she make just a mark on the page and see where that takes her. Vashti responds by jabbing her marker to the paper, producing a single dot. Her teacher asks Vashti to sign her painting and then puts it inside a frame and hangs it on the wall above her desk, and in so doing, she gives Vashti a new lens with which to regard her work. Her dot is now *framed as art* and, therefore, it *becomes* art. Vashti goes on to paint giant dots and multiple dots and dots of different colors, and she becomes a famous "dot painter" and gets an art show. So if we need to put a literal frame around a student's piece of writing in order to be able to regard it as art, then that is what we must do.

Recall the reflecting you did in Chapter 2—remember how we have lenses from our own schooling that make student writing ugly, that block out its beauty? We have voices in our heads and proofreading parrots on our shoulders endlessly repeating things like "subject/verb agreement" and "pronoun antecedents," that give us a tin ear for the music of kids' language. I wish I could erase those lenses and voices from our pasts so that we can read and revalue our students' writing for its true literary gifts. I yearn for everyone in the world to listen to the music in kids' writing and focus our eyes on its originality, its vibrant and playful use of new words and multiple languages, the way it collides with and borrows from multiple literacies: art, music, TV, movies, and games. I wish everyone could slow down and take the time to regard children's writing as art, especially the work of the many, many kids who don't fit into the square boxes that education values, the kids who produce the sparest pieces, the most obviously unreadable, or the most unappealing or uninteresting to us.

I want to read their dozens of video game reenactments for the high drama and zippy dialogue. I *need* to learn to like sports through their passionate, minutely detailed replays. I want to relish the hysterically funny ways kids see the world and be moved by their tenderheartedness, to take solace from their insights, and use their words to inspire. (On the wall by my computer, I have a collection of quotes from students' writing. One of my favorites is from one of my first graders: "Ms. Bomer tolldily lovs writing.") And yes, as a poet and essayist, I even want to copy or *remix* or *mash-up*, to use some lingo I recently learned, their phrases and images and stories for my own writing.

The Beauty of "Not the Way to Say It"

Let us begin to revalue student writing as literature with what I think is most appealing about student writing, and that is the unconventional way of saying things that most kids have. I delight, as all poets and writers delight, in unusual turns of phrase. Adult writers revise away from cliché and toward surprising words, phrases, metaphors, and images. Novelist Milan Kundera (author of *The Unbearable Lightness of Being*, among other brilliant texts) applauds translators who protect the "unusual and original formulations" of prose when transcribing it into another language (2000, 129). He claims he left a publishing company when they tried to change all his semicolons to periods. A writer reaches for what Kundera calls "not the way to say it" (a lovely, awkward way of putting it) on purpose. Young persons say things "not the way to say it" quite naturally. They are trying to name their world as they discover it, and they don't yet have the trite and conventional language for naming it, thank goodness! Their quirky wording, descriptions, and understandings move me to tears sometimes. In their unschooled—and as yet unencumbered by safe, hiding-from-the-truth, polite, or acceptable—language they have touched the fire, the quick, the heart of the matter. Remember Tyrell's writing from Chapter 1? His invented words and odd syntax have floated into my mind over the last ten years; my favorites are: "a wedding of somewhat incandescent value" and "his past as a child was a burning ship in no mercy."

In the beginning of his novel, *Atonement*, Ian McEwan gave his main character, a precocious eleven-year-old writer name Briony, this special quality of naming the world the way a child would:

> Her efforts received encouragement. In fact, they were welcomed as the Tallises began to understand that the baby of the family possessed a strange mind and a facility with words. The long afternoons she spent browsing through diction- ary and thesaurus made for constructions that were inept, but hauntingly so: the coins a villain concealed in his pocket were "esoteric," a hoodlum caught stealing a car wept in "shameless auto-exculpation," the heroine on her thor- oughbred stallion made a "cursory" journey through the night, the king's fur- rowed brow was the "hieroglyph" of his displeasures. (2003, 6)

When we were traveling in Japan, Randy and I delighted over the English writing on T-shirts (apparently, it's extremely popular to have English writing on your body somewhere), store names, and the occasional sign translated to English. The trans- lations said things differently than a native speaker of English would. My favorite name over a restaurant, for instance, said, "Please . . . Coffee." I asked Randy, do you think this is an ultra polite way of saying, "Come in and buy some coffee?" Does it mean, "We sell coffee that is *pleasing* to the taste buds?" Because I'm a coffee addict, I like to think they captured the words straight from my brain each and every morn- ing: "PLEASE . . . COFFEE!!"

The Brilliance of Kids' Passions

This idea of delighting in our kids' "not-the-way-to-say-it" writing has profound implications for many of our most reluctant, disinterested, and disenfranchised students. Another aspect of our students' writing that we can embrace is the topics and subjects they choose to write about when they truly have choice. When I taught fifth grade in Austin, Texas, a tight-knit group of boys in my class were fiends for Japanese anime. They practiced drawing the characters all over their notebooks, and it seemed that every entry in their writer's notebooks was a play-by-play of Dragonball Z. I accepted this. I told them they could write about anime to their heart's content, as long as they were practicing some of the writing strategies I taught in minilessons and writing conferences. The boys tried out anime poems, anime movie scripts; they invented new video games. When we were learning how to write feature articles, Joshua chose as his topic the history and popularity of . . . Japanese anime.

In *Boy Writers*, Ralph Fletcher makes a powerful case for teachers learning to take heart in the interest in gross things, bodily functions especially, the sometimes rough or dangerous language use, and even the inclusion of violence in the writing of many of the boys in our classrooms. "Encourage him to use words and phrases that sound like him. Allow him to do the writing only he can do. Let him see you react to and enjoy his writing" (2006, 167). It is the greatest gift you can give, Fletcher assures us.

We all have our limits for what is acceptable to our values, our sensitive eyes and ears, and our job security. Some people can handle the word *turd* and others can't. Some readers may wish I had elevated the word to *excrement,* but *turd* is what the boy wrote! I've engaged in serious and critical conversations in workshops with teachers about what we mean when we say, "You can write about anything you want to in your writer's notebook." In many places I work around the country, kids have questioned our sincerity when what they want and need to write about is neighborhood or family violence or participating in gang activities. Some teachers feel these topics are off-limits for school settings, while others express that their students would simply not write at all if they couldn't write rap songs, use gangsta language, and tell about the chaos they honestly experience every day, unimaginable as it may be to most of us. For teachers concerned about appropriate limits of language and topics in student writing, I suggest a four-pronged approach to figuring out some guidelines:

1. Find out the exact wording in your *state law* for reporting verbal and/or written statements regarding violence or abuse toward self or others.
2. Next, find out the exact wording of any *district* policy regarding topic and language in student writing.
3. Next, find out the exact wording of any *individual school* policy about same.
4. Finally, decide what your personal tolerance level is for topics and/or language use and either state that clearly upfront or deal with it only as it arises in individual cases.

I do not have the answers for how far we let kids go in their writing in schools, but I believe strongly that we lose legions of young people when we disavow what they know and care about. I worked in a seventh-grade class once where the teacher warned, before the observing teachers and I went in, that this group was the "lowest in the school." Several kids had been held back more than once, several were labeled "special education" students; and they sometimes arrived and sometimes did not for an English class that met at the final period of the day. Heavy, purple basal literature textbooks sat on the desks—the kind that would break your foot if one fell on it. I had that same purple textbook thirty-five years ago! If I had not appeared that day, the kids were going to be studying gerunds and participial phrases.

Before going into the class to demonstrate a lesson about choosing something to write about in their writer's notebook, I asked if I could interview a few kids about their writing lives. Noelle, soon to turn fifteen, and trapped in the seventh grade, told me that at home, she writes all the time. "What do you write?" I asked.

"Poems. My diary. I even write songs."

"Songs!" I was intrigued—a writing life teeming with life.

"Yeah, and I make up tunes and sing them on my guitar," she said.

"What about in school?" I asked.

"Here, writing is boring . . . it's about essays, you know? Paragraphs and like that. I don't feel my writing at school. I don't *feel* it, ya know? At home I know what I'm doing when I write."

Home was where writing was fun, alive, worthwhile, where she *knew what she was doing*. School was a place to put on a mask, be angry, and fail. And the minute we walked back into her classroom for my lesson, Noelle's face took on the angriest mask you can imagine. Had she been given the chance to write what interested her, she might have been able to learn something about writing, about revising and making her writing clear for an audience. This was a young woman who was not going to give a moment of attention to a lesson on gerunds and participial phrases.

A Quick Look at Some Excerpts from Student Writing

For the next few pages, I offer an overview of what I mean by the delightful snippets of young people's writing, the kinds of lines or sentences that teachers easily find when I ask them to look through their kids' work to read aloud some places they admire. Here, we will simply celebrate. This will give us some practice naming qualities with long language.

Ray,* Fourth Grade

> When it was time to take them to the vet [My dogs] Riley and Shelby didn't care. They didn't like or hate the vet.

What Do I See in This Piece of Writing?

Ray wrote an exquisitely detailed five-page narrative about his passion, his dogs, that unfortunately had to be taken back to the pound; apparently they were a bit unruly. But over and over he portrays them as cool, beneficent, playful, and beloved. I love his character portrait: "They didn't like or hate the vet." So funny to imagine because if you've ever taken a pet to the veterinarian, you know they simply aren't that "cool" about it.

Tyler, Fourth Grade

> The two dogs restroom in the house and they get yelled at.

What Do I See in This Piece of Writing?

Another passionate dog story; this time it's that terrific phrase with a noun I've never seen used as a verb before: "The two dogs *restroom* in the house." It's so polite!

Yesenia, Eighth Grade

> Ok, this isn't like a story that has happy endings or starts with once upon a time, and ends with happily ever after. This is a different story, like me you might say.

What Do I See in This Piece of Writing?

This is the opening paragraph that my friend Gaby Layden asked if she could read aloud to the group of teachers looking at student work. Gaby recognized immediately the literary quality, the sophistication of claiming at the start of a story that this one is not like all others, that it will not begin the same or end happily. This beginning intrigues the reader immediately. It doesn't use a sound effect, or a random bit of dialogue, or a description of the setting. Rather, it takes all our favorite lessons about good leads and flips them on their heads.

---

*All names are pseudonyms.

Masato, Fourth Grade

the dry up worms

when I walk to school. I pass by
light ble apartment house

I see something brown. I look more
near. there are dry up worms.

I think why lots of wormes are dryup?

I understand why they are dry up.
because worms creeped out when
sprinkler worked. then worms
failed to get in soil.

So they lost there lives.
poor worms.

The Dry Up Worms

When I walk to school I pass by light blue apartment house. I see something broun. I look more near. There are dry up worms.

I think why lots of worms are dry up? I understand why because worms creeped out when sprinkler worked. Then worms failed to get in soil so they lost their lives. Poor worms.

What Do I See in This Piece of Writing?

Every time I declare that a certain piece of writing is my most favorite, along comes another one to wear that mantle. This boy's writing reminds me of one of my favorite poets, Mary Oliver. In my mind, I see this alert and deeply sensitive young man, stopping to "look more near" (that quote now resides on the wall by my computer, by the way), mesmerized by the tiniest life outside, wondering why the worms are dried up and hypothesizing brilliantly about the answer. I love the way he words it: "the worms failed to get in soil." I have this image of earthworms struggling across vast expanses of concrete driveway. As soon as Masato directs my attention to this sad aspect of nature in suburbia, I think, "Yes! I've seen those worms too and wondered that. Thank you for reminding me to look and wonder again."

It's true that Masato's is just the kind of writing that I fret over when I'm in a harried frame of mind: the verb endings, the missing prepositions, the syntax, all are markers of a student who is learning English as an additional language. Masato is learning English; his first language is Japanese. As is often the case with many students like him, the brilliance of Masato's thinking could remain hidden because I'm so trained to find errors and worried about how he will pass the writing test in March. But again, I take a step back. I relax. And I read like an artist, digging for what is there. It would be a sin not to see Masato's amazing and compassionate mind at work behind the unconventional syntax.

Evan, Seventh Grade

Sometimes, I just can't concentrate on what I need to do. I just only want to watch the big game or go outside. I always know that if I do such and such now, I get to do this and that later. It is like having a map through a cave but no flashlight. I get lost so many times and sometimes just forget to do it all. It helps to have someone to guide you through the dark, and maybe they'll bring a flashlight. Someone to tell you, "keep steady," or "almost there." It sometimes is hard to be level-headed when you need help. Like the Beatles song, "With a Little Help from My Friends."

What Do I See in This Piece of Writing?

As Evan's stunning writing teacher, Betsy Kelly, wrote to me, "This is a gorgeous [underlined twice] reflection," to which I will add, "Amen." This little thought-piece is a perfect example of when a young person writes something that succinctly describes the human condition, and you want to say, "How do you know that yet, you're only a child!" Here's more from Evan:

I have noticed that I write faster in pen. I don't know why, but like in the poem, "The Pen," the pen is the weapon to capture the world with. My writing may be sloppier, my thoughts less detailed, but it is so much easier.

I also noticed that people pay to advertise for someone. Cars have the logo, Nike stuff has the check, McDonald's buys cups with the label, "Coca-Cola," on them. To me, this is proof the economy rules American, not good ideas or justice. Politicians who can sell themselves and get people to buy their cause. Democracy might as well now be a business, not a government.

Evan has an almost anarchistic energy in his writing voice, a revolutionary impulse. He does such important intellectual work in his writing; he is willing to entertain rather difficult, unsettling thoughts for a seventh grader, as you'll see in the next two entries.

> The first time I cared about politics was in fourth grade right around election. The whole grade was in turmoil, friends arguing over little things, people who disliked each other to the extreme acting like best of friends, and even a rumor about a fight that broke out between a republican and a democrat. Boys joked that they would *kiss a girl* if Ralph Nadar won, and girls said they would shave their head if Nadar succeeded. I tried to be suttle and be moderate democratic. After a week, I was in the heat of the fire, chanting and posting signs saying Kerry, Edwards '04. Close to election day, the girls kept civil, or at least in view of the boys and teachers. The boys, on the other hand were breaking out in arguments all the time. Though the Republicans were outnumbered in our school, Bush repeated and the Democrats were devastated. For weeks and weeks or maybe a day, Republicans would taunt the Democrats, sullen and blown away. But over time, civility was restored in the hallways, wrongs were healed, and bridges were rebuilt. The Republicans' swagger wore off like bad bug spray, and labels like donkey-lover (but with different wording) faded into the air and the good life was back.

Whew! Evan is one of those kids who I think can write circles around me. No matter what our political persuasion might be, we can't help but admire this honest and evocative reconstruction of a fourth-grade classroom's foray into the election season of 2004. I admire Evan's strong control of language and rhetoric: "civility restored/bridges rebuilt," "swagger." And I am jealous, I tell you, of the image of something wearing off "like bad bug spray," which brings to mind a horrible smell as well as frustration at its uselessness in combating mosquitoes—bad for two reasons. Brilliant. Just one more entry from Evan:

> Everyday, I think about what happens when I'm gone. Is it just like turning off a light or do I float on? Do I get reincarnated or do I live with God? I hate thinking about it but it just comes. Maybe unconsciously I like it, so I keep going back to it. I think everybody wonders about this. Most religions cover this. Science keeps trying to find the answer. I don't think I'll ever know, but within my life time they may figure out eternal life or body switching or maybe realistic space travel where weeks go by like days and decades like weeks. But maybe there is no answer, just nothing.

Evan writes with a philosopher's voice, asking the most profound and existential questions of life. Evan writes with an essayist's voice, letting one question or thought lead to another, exploring this idea and that idea about the afterlife. His mind is hugely expansive. It travels through space and time, across large cultural and religious concepts.

Evan's voice is poetic, especially in the end, where it gathers up phrases: "where weeks go by like days and decades like weeks," and then ends with the best word for an ending for this existential kind of writing that I've ever seen, except in the novels and plays of Samuel Beckett: "nothing." And then nothing comes after that, just white space. It's final and deeply scary.

Joyce, Seventh Grade

> I sat there in the same chair that was horribly uncomfortable and waited to see my grandma the way she always looked. Big sparkly blue eyes, almost silver hair and her lepperd print eye glasses. She only wore them indoors because she says that they make her feel fancy.

What Do I See in This Piece of Writing?

This excerpt is the first paragraph of a narrative about a car accident that a grandmother was involved in. In a revision, Joyce had brilliantly moved this from where it was buried in the middle of the story, to the opening scene. Joyce wrote this narrative in the first two days of the year as a benchmark assessment that we're working with in the middle and high schools of Sunnyside, Washington. After seeing Joyce's beginning-of-the-year writing, I am so grateful that she is in Jonathan Babcock's seventh-grade classroom because he is a writer, and he constantly celebrates what his students know and can do in writing.

It is evident that Joyce already understands when and how to use detail. While the character sits in the hospital waiting room for news about her beloved grandmother's condition, she tries to bring her image to mind—the way she "always looked" (because after the accident, she might now look differently). Joyce chooses only three concrete items to describe the grandmother: eyes, hair, and glasses, and gives them specificity in the adjectives: *sparkly* blue, *almost* silver (love that) and *leopard* print. And oh, I had to read that last sentence out loud to several people, ". . . they make her feel fancy." Oh my, yes.

Sam, Fourth Grade

On a chilly October morning I drowsily opened my eyes and saw a blue creature. My eyes adjusted and instead I saw my sister in blue pajamas. She was at my plain bedroom door. She was now standing over me ready to bore me to death. Then she whispered, "let's play the ps2." I gritted my teeth and answered "Its a school day." "No its not" said my sister smudgly. "Now get up lazy." "Get out and don't come back," I yelled as she went out the door. Then I thought, this is every day life with her."

What Do I See in This Piece of Writing?

Oh, how I love Sam's sarcastic voice! This paragraph from his personal narrative draft could be the opening of a novel by any of our favorite children's literature writers, and it would immediately grab the attention of its readers. In the first sentence, I read with a touch of dread, I must admit, not being a fan of science fiction or fantasy: a blue creature. But no—that's his sister! And we're off and running, anticipating more diatribes against this smug (do we care one iota that a nine-year-old misspelled *smugly*? No, we do joyful back flips over that perfect word) person he has to put up with.

The dialogue is pitch-perfect between this brother and sister. It's Lucy and Linus. It's the big sister and little brother in *Ira Sleeps Over* by Bernard Waber. Don't you love the world-weariness of that last line: "this is every day life with her," sigh.

And so you see, most of us might be used to beginning in weakness—misspelled words, endless, winding sentences, lack of a logical organization, lack of paragraphs. But with practice, it becomes easier to begin in strength if we take the time to admire new text forms, to find unusual words and images, and life experiences and points of view vastly different from our own, and to appreciate particular skills like sarcasm, humor and hyperbole, naturalistic dialogue, graphic skills, and expression of deep feeling. From there, our teaching points will fall on eager, alert, excited ears. In the next chapter, I take us through some longer student pieces, several of which have serious writing issues, and list a few possibilities for what else I would teach those students after I have taught them what they already do so well.

How Can Generous and Careful Reading of Student Writing Tell Us What to Teach?

Exploring Student Writing with New Lenses

In this chapter, I provide alternatives to those "reading with dread" scenarios that teachers feel when facing piles of student writing to assess. I offer a variety of samples from students ranging from ages eight to fifteen, from diverse socioeconomic and language backgrounds, from urban, rural, and suburban settings. When I have factual information, or when it feels appropriate to include a student's family or life circumstance, I do so. I have purposely included the kind of writing that causes all of us to scratch our heads in bewilderment. These pieces vary in length, structure, genre, and technical ability. Many of them fit the common issues that cause teachers to despair: brevity, lack of concrete images and details, confusing sentence structures, and language conventions errors.

I attempt in the following examples to name at least three things I can find to compliment about these pieces of writing. Following the section where I name what each student does well as a writer, I list two or three possible directions for where I could imagine taking my teaching of each in writing conferences. You will notice that the directions are most often large, comprehensive, almost theatrical in nature, rather than isolated tips for fixing up the piece in front of me. I attempt, as Lucy Calkins suggests, to grow the *writer*, not the *writing*, a distinction that I hope my teaching ideas will help clarify. The lenses I see through, the language I know to say in response to student writing, and the ideas I share for what to teach next come from reading, writing, and learning from writers and artists how to talk about art.

But as Mary Dentrone, literacy coach at PS 199 in Queens, says, "Teachers shouldn't worry about needing to talk like a published writer; the most important thing is you should want to say something as if you care, as a person." While our first response to the physical look of several of these student pieces might be to sigh or throw our hands up in despair of even being able to read them, remember to relax, sit next to me, and let's journey together to find the beauty and brilliance that is there. Let's read them as if we care, as persons.

Reading Student Writing with a Writer's Eye and Ear

Christopher, Fourth Grade

I was worid decos I thot that I will not git ho presents on crismas a ncrismas was going to be tomorow then the next day it was my luke day decos I got a puch of presents I got my presents I got my presents tata tatata now it is thim to party.

Disco

I was worried because I thought that I will not git no presents on Christmas, and Christmas was going to be tomorrow. Then the next day it was my lucky day because I got a bunch of presents.
I got my presents,
I got my presents,
Tata, tata, tata, ta.
    (sung to the tune of "La Cucaracha")
Now it is time to party!

Who Is This Child?

Christopher is a twin. Both boys arrived in the United States from Mexico, at least one year prior to this piece of writing. They have both moved in and out of foster care (together, as far as I know), and at the time that I met them, they had settled into one foster home. Chris is by far the more gregarious of the two; his brother hides behind Chris and peers around him. Chris wants everyone to read his writing, or better yet, to listen as he performs it out loud. His writing often contains bits of popular songs to which he writes new lyrics that have to do with the topic of the piece.

What Do I See in This Piece of Writing?

This excerpt is from Christopher's writer's notebook entry as practice for responding to state writing test prompts. The prompt for this entry was "Write a composition about a time you were worried about something or someone."

Chris presents surprisingly honest feelings for a nine-year-old boy. He is worried about not getting any presents on Christmas. This is not an idle fear; he has lived in many houses in his young life, and moved away from his home and family in Mexico. Nothing has been stable for him, and several Christmases have come and gone without presents. That he can write about this with such a sense of humor and fun is a testament to his personal strength. The humor also helps the piece rise above sentimentality, and that has the strange effect, for me, of making the situation even sadder. Thinking of his spunk and perseverance in the face of his situation moves all the adults who know him.

This piece expresses tension and suspense: *I thought that I will not git no presents for Christmas.* He doesn't end there, but adds: *and Christmas was going to be tomorrow.* This first sentence immediately draws the reader into the drama of the situation. We can all remember that childhood anticipation of presents at holidays. Most of us cannot relate to a fear that there might not actually *be* any presents awaiting us. I admire the restraint with which Chris explains the situation. I picture this little boy, trying not to cry, carrying the weight of the world on his shoulders, but never complaining. Our impulse would be to ask him to thoroughly dramatize the drama for us, to tell us the whole, sad background story of his life. There might be a time and place for that, but in this piece, he lets a world of grief hide behind the words, "I thought I will not git no presents on Christmas." Again, what is *not* said in this case oddly increases the pathos for me.

There is a hint of time passing, letting us know that one day there was worry, the next day there was joy and relief from worry. It expresses a classic narrative contrast, "It used to be, but now. . . ."

The choice of the word *lucky*, again, breaks my heart. Inside of only two sentences, I get a sense of the character of this narrative. Consciously or not, Chris portrays himself as a person without expectations for how life is supposed to go, but considers himself "lucky" when it goes well. He might have written, "But then I didn't worry anymore because I did get a bunch of presents." That would have revealed less about his particular character than does the word, *lucky*. Although some teachers cringe at the word, *bunch*, thinking that it sounds like slang or it is not specific enough about what kinds of presents, but it fits this character, and it sounds like a word that a child would use. The same goes for the last line, "Now it is time to party!" For a child fearing no gifts, the appearance of gifts signals a time for celebration, or in young people's parlance, "time to party!"

Chris is a performer in his writing. He hears songs and does not hesitate to pull actual music into the thread of his narrative. He chooses an appropriately joyful, funny tune, to match his surprise and relief that indeed, there were presents for him on Christmas, and he cleverly rewrites the lyrics of "La Cucaracha" (of all songs!) to fit his purpose; the literary term for this is *parody*, and is truly a literary skill.

Finally, his teacher need not worry about Chris knowing how to answer the writing prompt on state tests. He responds precisely to the practice test prompt, which was "Write about a time when you were worried about something or someone." He answers the question in the very first sentence, assuring that he can find things to write about when given even such a general prompt.

Possible Directions for Teaching Chris

1. I would teach directly into Chris' desire to perform for an audience. I would ask him who in the classroom he feels comfortable with to be his writing partner, or perhaps set him up in a writing club with two or three friends. Each day, Chris needs an opportunity to read his writing out loud and get instant response to it. That response needs to grow from the initial naming of what he does well to a request for clarity and consistency (staying with one event or topic over the course of several days), and then I would request that his writing group make a contract with each other so that each other's suggestions for revision will get filled.

2. I would expand the genre possibilities for Chris to explore. I could imagine him becoming quite excited to write anything that leads to a performance: a play or musical, a film script, a commercial, a podcast.

Trey, Fourth Grade, Special Education

My cat Shuggie. She was the nicest cat in the world. She would. She had to get put to sleep cuz she would not use the restroom at all. It was weird. And she would not eat at all. That was weird too. She slept with me. She was so cute.

Who Is This Child?

When Trey's loving fourth-grade teacher, Heather Hughes, handed me this piece of writing after my workshop with the upper-grade teachers in her school, she prefaced it with how proud she was of him—that this was the longest thing he had written, three months into the school year. Yet she still felt enormously frustrated, she admitted. She and Trey faced the fourth-grade state writing test, and his writing, at least at that time, would earn a zero.

What Do I See in This Piece of Writing?

I took the piece of paper and read it quietly out loud to myself, trying to work my way through the approximated spellings. I read it as I would read a poem, slowly, with emphasis on key words, and a slight lilt of my voice at the end of each sentence. By the time I reached the sentence "She slept with me," I was literally in tears. Why did this piece get to me? I must have twenty "dead pet" student writing pieces in my files, and some are truly captivating. But the simplicity of this one, and the mental image I had of Trey, a large nine-year-old boy, struggling to get these few words down, words from the very core of him, got to me.

I immediately said to Heather, "This same thing just happened to me this past summer! Exactly what he says here: '. . . she would not use the restroom at all; she would not eat at all.' My cat, Pearl, was only four years old and we had no idea why this was happening. We had to put our sweet cat to sleep too, and we could barely get through it."

I gushed on to the small group of teachers now huddled around Trey's piece. Look at that parallel structure: "She would not . . . at all"/"She would not . . . at all" and "It was weird"/"That was weird too." This piece was supposed to be a personal narrative, yet his narrative structure blows open the conventional notion of how a "story" goes. He uses time in a fluid and meaningful way. After Trey introduces the main focus of his story, Shuggie, he goes straight to the *end* of the story: "She had to be put to sleep." Then he goes further back in time to narrate what happened to the cat. We might imagine his family watching this cat and acting differently during this sad time, and saying this exact language about her.

The piece ends with what might normally be at the beginning of this kind of narrative. It might have gone: "My cat Shuggie was the nicest cat in the world. She was so cute. She used to sleep with me . . . ," and then proceed to tell the events of her illness and death in sequence. By ending instead with this image of her cuteness and her place beside Trey while he slept, all the grief that he *still* carries with him resides in those simple words. The words leave us, as readers, with the visceral image that remains of Shuggie's warmth next to his body in his most vulnerable times, while he slept.

Heather, his teacher, said that Trey has been miserable since Shuggie's death. She was in tears by this point also. I begged her for a copy of this piece, and while she was at the copy machine in the teachers room, it happened (as if by magic), that Trey's third-grade teacher came in. Heather told her what she was copying and why, and then his former teachers started crying. She said, "I remember Shuggie! Trey loved that cat!"

"Please go back and tell Trey that he made a group of teachers including his third-grade teacher cry over this little bit of writing," I said.

"Oh, I will," Heather promised. If she did that, I knew she would create a writer that day. Trey would know that writing reaches out to people and moves them, makes them cry and remember their own experiences with beloved pets.

This little story lives on. I showed the piece the very next day to another group of teachers at a *different* school, and one of them burst into tears, remembering her special pet, and had to leave the room. Several months later, when I returned to work at Trey's school, his principal, literacy coach, and several teachers warned me throughout the day that Trey knew I was in the building and he wanted to meet "that lady who likes my writing." Apparently, in between my first and second school visits, Trey had become an unstoppable writing force. He began writing poems, all about Shuggie, of course. I shook Trey's hand when I met him, and I said, "You are becoming quite the famous writer, Trey! I've shared your story about Shuggie with teachers all over the United States!"

Trey looked at me confidently and said, "And it's gonna be in your book too."

"That's right, it is!" I showed him what it would look like by showing him some of the student writing that appears in my book, *Writing a Life* (2005).

"Can I have that book?" Trey asked. His teacher and I laughed and said, "We've created a reading and writing monster!"

Possible Directions for Teaching Trey

1. Since Trey remains clearly obsessed with his beloved cat, Shuggie, I could imagine him launching an all-out Shuggie retrospective. He could make a scrapbook with captions beneath photographs and drawings and little anecdotes of life with his cat. He could take that online and make a digital story or PowerPoint presentation all about that cat.

2. Trey's gift for touching people might truly shine in smaller texts that can give him more control over fewer words: poems, greeting cards, picture books. I would introduce Trey to poetry and suggest that he write a poem a day (this is an exercise that I give myself, so I know how it can benefit) to help with his writing fluency. His knack for repetition and parallelism ("she would not"; "that was weird too") has ancient precedent in oral and written poetry. I would show Trey several samples of this from poems for kids that he might like. Those samples might become models for his poems.

Lucelia, Fifth Grade

She Shoots . . . I Fall

When that bell rang everyone went CRAZY! The guys were insane! They let out huge yells and girlish screams. I'd do it too because that is our only signal to have as much fun as possible, until another bell rings and we have to go back to class.

I jumped out of my seat and told Christy, my best friend, to get a ball. I headed towards the door, jumped over a backpack that was on the floor, made my way through the crowd and out the door.

Christy was already ahead of me! I trotted over and said, "Race ya" and I sprinted ahead.

At first I ran all heavy, my feet pumping on the ground so hard I thought I left dents in the black concrete. But then I ran smoother and faster. I felt the wind blow my hair away from my face. I felt faster than a cheetah. But a cheetah runs for its prey, so I ran to beat Christy AND to get a good court too.

. . . I see Christy make a perfect shot! I give Christy a mean look, and she just smiles. Then she bounces the ball all around the court laughing like she is the happiest person on the face of the earth.

Then she stops and got ready to shoot again. But I am too fast and quickly block her. She pretends to shoot left, and I foolishly block her left and then she skidded around me and shoots.

We looked at the ball. My heart pumping faster and faster, my legs and fingers crossed. My mouth moving to the words "don't make it . . . don't make it."

Christy's hands still in position. Everything seemed like it was in slow motion . . . the ball . . . my heart. My foot was cocked to the right. I felt gravity is pushing on my left.

Then suddenly my foot gave up, time went fast. My heart stopped for a while, then I fell on the ground scraping my arm and hands. Both of my hands clutched my knee, tears falling down my cheeks, my body on the hard concrete floor. My eyes closed and my face turned bright red.

. . . I didn't know much at that time. I couldn't really see, hear or think. I didn't know if the ball made it, I didn't know that Christy was patting my back and telling me it's o.k. All I knew was that I was hurt.

I studied my ankle to see if it was o.k. Then I looked up and saw all of my friends take one glance at me and come running one by one towards me . . .

. . . My crying was more like a sniffle now. And a few hours later, my ankle was back to normal. It was so easy to get over this because I had a lot of friends helping me.

What Do I See in This Piece of Writing?

I don't know Lucelia. I do know her fantastic teacher, Julieanne Harwitz from San Pedro, California, who kindly sent this piece to me. If I had not seen Lucelia's name as the author, I would have assumed a young man wrote this basketball narrative. Oh how I love it when my assumptions crumple to the floor!

Lucelia appears to be the kind of student writer who stumps us because she is so skilled that it's hard to know what to teach her beyond fixing some verb tenses or to make new paragraphs when a new person talks. Occasionally, we resort to a lame, "Do you have any questions for me?" We know that she soaks up the content of our minilessons about powerful verbs (Lucelia uses *trotted, stole, tossed, blocked, bounces, skidded* on the first page alone), and knows how to self-assess, revise, and edit, so we leave her alone to tend to all the other kids in our class who need so much help.

Look at that opening moment. Everyone, even the guys, lets out "girlish screams." That's such a true, perfect way to name that sound. "Our signal to have as much fun as possible until another bell rings and we have to go back to class." Ouch! Again, so honest that it hurts my teacher-heart. This narrator has reeled me in to this story already with her true perspectives. She envisions herself so completely inside the classroom in that moment that she can add this priceless detail: "I jumped over a backpack that was on the floor. . . ."

I also don't know if Julieanne typed this story or if Lucelia did; either way, some of the mistakes might be typos; I make them constantly, so I do not want to assume that some things are "not the way to say it" if they are only not the way to type it. But there are several places when Lucelia proves she is merely a fourth grader and not a young adult novelist, Chris Crutcher or Matt de la Peña, in disguise.

The paragraphs that describe her fall, beginning with "We looked at the ball" and ending with "my face turned bright red," are lovely, but also odd. I think only a kid would say, "my legs and fingers crossed." It's hard to get a firm grip on what the actions are between "my foot was cocked to the right" and "gravity is pushing on the left," and which foot "gave up."

Yet I would probably not change one word of those three paragraphs. Yes, I would absolutely leave in the fragment, "Christy's hands still in position." You *would* see that in a Crutcher novel, as you would also see the sophisticated, alliterative twist of "my mouth moving to the words 'don't make it . . . don't make it.'" Wow. As with the detail of jumping over the backpack in the first scene, Lucelia relives this moment so tightly that she remembers to put the ball and her heart (!) in slow motion as she falls and then makes time go fast again after the fall. That is what it feels like to fall, isn't it?

There are a dozen things I could say that Lucelia does well as a writer, but still, we can teach her more. Here are some ideas I have; keep in mind that I don't know Lucelia and have only this one narrative to go by.

Possible Directions for Teaching Lucelia

1. One of my favorite writing lessons concerns the endings of texts. Endings are hard, even for competent writers like Lucelia, and it takes time to get the feel of a good ending reverberating inside writers' heads. I would tell Lucelia that as a reader, her ending cannot hold a candle to all that comes before it. It's as if she knows the "good part" is the fall and the pain, and once we know she's alive and well (her ankle is not even broken, it turns out), she's got to rush off the stage. She could make the ending work as hard as the rest of the piece does; in her original, unex-

cerpted narrative, it takes five paragraphs just to get to the court; four to fall; and about fourteen to show her friends responding to her fall! Her last line is lovely, but she could make more of this. She could do what I call "read in reverse," to see if this is a thread she could tie up better by adding in more things about friendship throughout the entire piece. (I've written many more ideas about how to teach endings in my book about memoir, called *Writing a Life* [2005].)

2. If Lucelia is into sports as much as this narrative would lead me to believe, I might possibly line her up with stacks of sports writing to study: novels, poems, feature articles, and newspaper columns. I would let her discover what kind of writing thrills her the most and instruct her to practice as much as possible writing like that. Then I would ask for her autograph for when she becomes a famous female sportswriter.

Jacques, Ninth Grade

I am from where lil AKA Black drive around town in that Lex
while Slim in the front while me and Wennie is in the back
and Young Roc and Ed at Killa Man's house
while Blaze and Round playing Madden on the Xbox or the p.s.3.
I am from where Desire's girl Deedy and New New fight in
their room because they are not agreeing with each other right now.
I am from where grandma cooks fish and chicken on Friday
and on Sunday you know she is cooking a big meal.
I am from where you see nice funerals. Big TVs and pictures on the wall.
I am from where on August 29, 2005 Hurricane Katrina hated.
And where when it hit I had to leave all dat behind.
I am from New Orleans.

Who Is This Child?

Jacques was one of the thousands of kids who were transplanted by families or by city and state governments to cities in Texas after Hurricane Katrina destroyed their homes in New Orleans on August 29, 2005. Jacques and his mom were sent to Austin, and he was in my friend Deb Kelt's ninth-grade English class. Deb told me that he was a tough boy and sad to be away from his family and friends.

What Do I See in This Piece of Writing?

This excerpt is from Jacques' longer imitation of George Ella Lyon's poem, "Where I'm From." I have shown Jacques' amazing poem to hundreds of teachers in the last few years, and they are always moved by it and generous with their comments. They can hear the honesty and the humor in his expression, and they feel the pain of his missing his hometown after the devastating hurricane. While we may not understand all the music and pop culture references, we feel the absolute necessity of those precise nouns and verbs spelled in those exact ways. This is Jacques' voice, and he does not need any lessons on how to get more of it.

At a workshop in Austin, Texas, I asked Deb Kelt to read this poem out loud for the audience. I had been mangling the rhythms and sounds every time I'd read it to audiences, and now I could enlist Deb's help. She read it with all the love and memory she has for Jacques, and the audience was more visibly and audibly moved than ever. Teachers said that Jacques' language was "unapologetic," that he used a special dialect for the place he wrote about, as Mark Twain did in his novels. One teacher called Jacques' descriptions "crisp" in the simplicity of "they are not agreeing with each other right now." It is crisp and so funny too. Teachers noticed that the specific, precise names of things, "Lex" and "Xbox" and his list of "ghetto" nicknames, provided instant setting in time and place without paragraphs of flowery descriptions. They loved the language that was unknown to them set against such familiar words as *fish*, and *chicken*, and then unfortunately the word everyone now knows, *Katrina*, which again, does not need a paragraph of description, but carries the force of impact in just one name.

I love how Jacques' poem is full of those quirky, "not-the-way-to-say-it" words and phrases. Of course, it *is* the way to say it for Jacques and his friends in New Orleans, but I love the self-confidence he possesses to put those words on paper in a high school classroom. (He also knows that his teacher, Deb, will accept and encourage him to write from what he knows and cares about.)

When I first read that line: "I am from where . . . Hurricane Katrina *hated*," I thought it was the kind of quirky mistake that I relish in kids' writing, a slightly off way of saying "Hurricane Katrina hit" that perfectly described the indescribable. A teacher in a workshop kindly informed me that "hated" is what Jacques meant to say because "hating on" is a street expression meaning to intensely dislike someone. The Online Slang Dictionary (onlineslangdictionary.com) reports that the verb *hate on* refs specifically to being jealous, which would make his description of what Hurricane Katrina did to New Orleans even riper with meaning, given his love song to his hometown.

Possible Directions for Teaching Jacques

1. Since she is a brilliant, intuitive, and deeply compassionate teacher, I know that Deb probably did what I'm going to suggest here and more, but I'll list these possibilities anyway. I would suggest that Jacques list in his writer's notebook four or five "hot button" topics—things he is pretty sure he's "not allowed" to write about in school. After he lists a few—gangs, Tupac Shakur, naked bodies, whatever—I would set the timer and say, "Pick one and write about it for five full minutes, go!" Do this a few times until Jacques begins to see pages of prose grow under his fingertips.

2. As far as I'm concerned, Jacques is already a skilled, intelligent, moving poet. I would encourage him to find a few songwriters or poets whom he admires and can learn from. He could print appropriate lyrics and poems and collect them in a writing folder to have alongside as he writes his own poems. (For ideas about reading like a writer, see Chapter 3.)

Garett, Fourth Grade

Ike

"Oh no!" I got water in my house! I said. I whent to my room and my floor was wet. There was insultation every where! Thar was also a big pice of dry wall covering my dresser.

I was really afraid to go in house after Ike. I was very sad becouls I lost evr thang. I felt lik I was going to cry but I tride not to but it did not last very long. I started to cry I had lost my faverit stufft animal. I cep wondering if my house was ok. I had never expernst eny thang lik Ike.

On the radyo I hird the ruporter say that huston had a lot of damig and lots of fluding. I thot my house was gon becouls the ruporter said that part of the brig was flodid. My mom turnd it of mom I have't finsht listening to the rateo. I said I don't car. When you listen to the radiyo you have night mars and when you have night mars I cant sleep becols you tlak in your sleep said my mom.

Who Is This Child?

I worked in Garett's classroom in the Clear Creek School District south of Houston, just a few weeks after Hurricane Ike devastated entire swaths of Galveston and sections of the little towns north of Galveston where Clear Creek students live. Garett had been held back and was beginning his second stab at fourth grade. He was a small, slight boy, pale and timid, with cornflower blue eyes and hair the color of dandelion fluff. He seemed a bit traumatized, perhaps even in tears, the day I gave a minilesson in his class, and he refused to confer with me. I remember being quite upset by that because I don't usually have that kind of effect on kids. Jennifer Kessler, his knowledgeable and energetic teacher whose tone speaks volumes of love, brought me some of his work to read, and I found his piece called "Ike" so moving.

What Do I See in This Piece of Writing?

The first thing that leapt out at me from this piece was the confidence of Garett's voice, especially given how shy and scared he seemed in person. His writing voice is straightforward and remarkably restrained for such a frightening topic. I read quite a few "Ike" pieces in the months that followed that horrible storm, and many were unfortunately melodramatic and empty of visceral detail. It takes a mature control to write about extreme grief, pain, sadness, or fear without sounding overblown and somehow dishonest. The simple statement of fact—"I was sad because I lost everything"—is heartbreaking, more so because of its simplicity: what more can you say if you have lost everything?

Garett chooses two perfect concrete images to describe what a completely flooded house looks like. He might have said, "the walls fell down," but the picture of that nasty foam (that's what I see in my mind's eye) and a piece of actual wall fallen over his dresser make my mental picture microscopic in detail. Garett's use of almost technical language—*insulation, drywall, damage, reporter*—keeps the story grounded and factual, allowing the reader to fill in the emotion.

Garett has an honest voice, and for me, that instantly elevates a piece of writing; he is brave enough to admit not only that he had a favorite stuffed animal, but that he cried about losing it in the flood. My heart aches for this boy who worries about his house, and I can so easily picture him sitting right next to the radio, hungry for news of what is gone and what remains, refusing to turn the reports off, even though they give him "nightmares."

It is a smart narrative turn to let his mother be the one to divulge the news that he experiences nightmares instead of the first-person narrator ("When you listen to the radio, you have nightmares . . . and then I can't sleep . . ."). It's as if we have corroboration now—an eyewitness to the main character's suffering, without him saying it himself, so we trust the "I" more.

Finally, what makes this piece most memorable for me is one sentence: "I felt like I was going to cry but I tried not to but it did not last very long." I know that the syntax of this sentence is confusing, and if Garett would simply put a period after "cry" and delete the first "but," it would make more sense. He could clarify what did not last long, the crying or the trying *not* to cry? Perhaps I would teach him how to do that, after I make a big deal over the perfection of this sentence as a portrait of emotional and physical realism. Clive James, a literary critic with laser-beam intelligence, calls sentences like this an "ignition point for our attention" (2008, 483). It's the one word or image or odd sentence in the midst of ordinary prose that anyone could have written that bursts with energy because it is strange and perfect, once you read it, for what it says and where it comes in the text. We can forgive a bland string of prose sentences or unlyrical lines of poetry for that one odd place that begs to be read and reread. Garett's sentence is an "ignition point" for my attention because he has described, in his childlike way, exactly what it feels like to try hard to keep tears from flowing but not being able to stop them. Rather than words that would pass right over me: "I tried not to cry, but I couldn't stop crying," he wrote, "I tried not to but it did not last very long," *this trying not to*. That sentence makes my throat constrict every time I read it.

Possible Directions for Teaching Garett

1. Because Garett has already been flagged as a failure by our education system and because he is terrified, for whatever reason, of unfamiliar adults around him, my first step with Garett would be to take attention off any kind of high-stakes writing. I would have him working daily in his writer's notebook, and look for ways that he can share his writing in safe configurations—with a peer or small group of friends, by having someone else read it out loud the first few times, and by making a great deal out of the literary gifts that I mentioned.

2. I think that Garett has powerful visual memory for detail, so I would invite him to sketch and create storyboards for any kind of narrative writing he does. *Storyboards*,

because they are pictorial and sequential, often work better than timelines, which are merely word and number abstractions for many kids like Garett. They can flesh out the little boxes with graphic, visual details, then look at them and find words to name what is happening in the boxes. I would put one of the many graphic novels for kids directly into Garett's hands as soon as possible to show him how even in drawings, a narrative can be stretched to cover a whole novel-length book.

3. Garett appears to be an aural speller. He relies heavily on "sounding out" his spelling, and that is a weak strategy for most English words. So when he sounds out the word *there* he hears *thar*, and *anything*, he hears *eny thang*, because that is how he talks. I would work with him on a steadily growing list of words that he should know by heart such as *there* and *went*, using visual spelling strategies such as writing the word a few times to see which one looks right.

Jamal, Fourth Grade

Sparky promised to be nice. David held his pinky. Sparky held his pinky they shaked. With light coming down Yousef felt like a million dollars he felt as happy as if he earned a trillion bucks. Simon well you couldn't even put in words how happy he was. Before he left he said, "three words. best day ever". Yousef I have to tell you something I'm moving Yousef." Yousef started sobbing then it started to rain. Why I don't know no we just are." I'm sorry sparky I'm sorry to". Simon ran away before Yousef even said goodbye. Yousef fell on the ground crying and crying in the cold dark rain they never saw each other again.

Who Is This Child?

Jamal's teacher, Amber Boyd Vincent, and I were once colleagues at the Teachers College Reading and Writing Project. When she moved to Washington, DC, to become a fourth-grade teacher, all I could think was, "Oh, those lucky kids!" If there were ever a teacher who embodied, inside and out, the adjective *angelic*, it would be Amber. When she told me that her relationship with Jamal was strained, that he would not talk with her in a writing conference, that he would simply turn his back to her, I honestly could not believe it. But that is how destroyed Jamal was, even as a fourth grader, from the previous responses in and perhaps out of school about the problems in his writing. Herrington and Curtis (2000), authors of *Persons in Progress*, note that sharing writing with others is often at best an embarrassment. Nothing leaves you as wide open for ridicule and judgment as putting your thoughts and feelings on paper for unappreciative audiences to read. But when the response is cold or repulsed as incomprehensible student writing often elicits, the result for the writer is *shame*. And the by-product of shame, Herrington and Curtis write, is "often incoherent rant or, more often, abject silence" (210). This is the place where Amber found Jamal.

Amber and I looked together at Jamal's realistic fiction narrative. At first, I could not read it. There were shifts in verb tense and from third to first person, and changes in character's names, sometimes all on the same page. The punctuation was occasional and usually unhelpful. As soon as I put my voice to it, with Amber helping decipher some words, the sentences not only made sense but became lively and funny, demonstrative, and ultimately terribly sad.

I picked up some other pieces of writing from Jamal's portfolio and saw the same labored handwriting (I would wager a bet that he came from a school that focused on handwriting to the detriment of all other aspects of composition), the same muddled syntax and confused punctuation. I spent a few more minutes reading and rereading. What spoke clearly to me was Jamal's profound attention to relationships. On almost every piece of paper, there were play-by-plays of greeting friends, protecting each other from fights and bullying, and of losing strong friendships because of moving to another state. I said to Amber, "This child is a genius at social and emotional relationships! They pervade his thinking and writing, to the exclusion of almost everything. It is so hard to write well about deep friendships without sounding sentimental and sappy, and he is doing it with one of the most sophisticated literary techniques— letting the physical environment stand for his emotional environment. Look here at this ending: 'Yousef started sobbing, then it started to rain.' The external exactly matches the internal. Then finally, 'Yousef fell on the ground crying and crying in the cold dark rain.' Now the tears are pouring, as is the rain, *cold and dark*, as is loneliness. Such great drama! And that last sentence: 'They never saw each other again.' Definitely not a TV-movie-of-the-week ending, is it?"

Possible Directions for Teaching Jamal

Amber took these new things we saw in Jamal's writing back to the classroom with her and tried, at first unsuccessfully, to reach out to Jamal. Later, I received a handwritten letter from Amber in the mail, telling this moving and beautifully written ending to the story. Instead of the numbered list of teaching ideas I've included after all the other students, I believe that for Jamal, this letter offers the best teaching direction I could imagine giving to this young man.

A few days after you left, Jamal and I took a quiet moment with his writing portfolio. I shared with him that there had been some things I had missed, and that I wanted to compliment him. As the room quieted to work, Jamal joined me on the rug. "Come a little closer," I said. The distance he had placed between us made an intimate conversation nearly impossible. As he inched slowly toward me, I opened his portfolio to his realistic fiction piece. His body language had the cautious air of uneasiness. I explained to him that I had taken a moment with some other teachers to look at his writing. I said, "You know, sometimes I don't read students' work as carefully as I should and sometimes I miss the beautiful parts."

In the most candid comment Jamal ever made to me he said, "So you didn't even read my writing?" In one of those moments when time seemed to stand still, I realized Jamal is right, by not noticing and complimenting the beautiful parts of students' writing, I am not *really* reading it. I stammered a response and began my compliments. Like a plant thirsting for water, Jamal slowly drank it all in, his facial expression softened, and maybe just maybe one corner of his mouth twitched upward. I ended with, "Jamal, you came to our class uncomfortable with writing and look at you now. You are a writer!" The compliment conference ended soon after that without a verbal response from Jamal.

It was so great to give Jamal the compliments he deserved for his writing but better still, and more important, our relationship has improved. He is suddenly asking questions when he is confused, looking me in the eye when we talk, and allowing me in more to share in his life. He now sees himself as a writer with value, as a student who can achieve, and as a boy who is deeply cared about. Thank you for helping me see the diamonds in Jamal's rough writing.
Love,
Amber

A Final Invitation

When Randy and I went to Japan, we traveled to Hiroshima to see the Peace Memorial Park and the Peace Flame and the museum that houses the story of that horrible day, August 6, 1945, when the United States dropped the first atomic bomb, ultimately killing over 140,000 people. What I did not know until I read that history and saw the artifacts collected in the museum was that over 6,000 children died in that blast. I had to summon the full powers of my imagination to conjure that scene. Though I could not begin to do it justice (what from my own life can touch the chaos and horror of that?), I imagined enough to turn my stomach and stop my breath.

The day we visited, thousands of Japanese kids, a hundred busloads-full on field trips from all over the island, filled the park. In front of a memorial built to Sadako (whose moving story was made famous by Eleanor Coerr in *Sadako and the Thousand Paper Cranes*), we were approached again and again by groups of kids in fourth to

A Note on Working with Multilingual Students

I have been lucky to participate in a study group in Austin, Texas, with teachers of multilingual students. We call the students *multilingual* because, in fact, some of them use two, three, and four languages. This term immediately respects what they *know*, not what they don't know, as the words *English language learner* connotes. We also use multilingual, for want of an even more perfect label, because it seeks to respect the idea that rather than sporting a deficit in the English language, these kids possess multiple riches, more than many people born and educated in the United States, by knowing, speaking, reading, and writing in more than the language they learned as babies.

While we continue to introduce our students to conventional English, and while we explain that there are occasions that require conventional English, we also invite them to use, share, and study their home language for as long as they want or need to. In a writing classroom, the sharing of language similarities and differences provides everyone with a rich bank of language knowledge from which to draw.

In the writings of English learners, we must be careful to frame their "not-the-way-to-say-it" syntax and diction not as error, but as the gift it often is: a fresh and delightful perspective on the world, resulting from the transition from students' first language to English. A common example of this would be a sentence like "No sé nada," which is emphatic and correct in Spanish; but "I don't know nothing" would be marked incorrect in English because it contains a double negative. These diverse ways with words can make fascinating study and can multiply the possibilities of language, and their speakers and writers can appear wealthy, not deficient.

eighth grades, with clipboards, fulfilling an assignment to find someone to practice their English with. Of course, the boys interviewed Randy and the girls interviewed me. We knew it was an assignment because everyone had sheets of paper with the same words on it, and the kids had all memorized the same script to say to us in English:

Hello, my name is _____. (student said his/her name)

Where are you from? _____

Do you like Japan? _____

Will you write some peace words? _____

Have this peace crane, please.

I loved that last line so much, I memorized it and kept saying it for the rest of the day: "Have this peace crane, please." All the kids had been required, apparently, to fold little paper cranes, just like Sadako—little peace cranes to give to the "English" people they interviewed. Tadeshi, Hidako, Koji, and Ren asked Randy to "write some peace words," and I took a picture of them watching Randy write on their clipboard. Then the boys gave their cranes to Randy. His were a bit lopsided, crumpled, not as teeny or sharply folded as the ones the girls gave to me.

When Randy got the crane that was perhaps the least perfectly shaped, a bit gray where the boy had run his fingers quickly over the folds, his shoulders shook, and I knew he was beginning to cry. When Randy is moved by anything involving children, I start to cry. Those poor kids; they must have wondered what the heck was going on—these two middle-aged Americans weeping in front of them.

One of the kids' teachers came up to me, and she had tears in her eyes too. She said, "Thank you for coming so far to see this monument. I can see you are moved. Thank you for coming here." Of course that made me cry even harder. We were in a veritable crying fest. I was a wreck for the rest of that afternoon, and we hadn't even gotten to the museum yet.

I invite all of us to be moved by our children's slightly off, a bit crumpled and unconventional offerings, as Randy was moved by the boy's paper crane. Let us look carefully and with generosity past what is missing and what is incorrect, to the extraordinary beauty, freshness, and yes, the brilliance in children's writing. Believe that children are trying to make something. That they have intentions, purposes, and reasons for writing the way they do.

"Have this peace crane, please."

8

What Can We See in Student Writing When We Read It with Colleagues?

I have a mental picture, perhaps you recognize a similar image, of the lonely English teacher at home in front of the television, or on the bus or subway to and from work, poring over endless, fabulously dull or pompous essays, hunting for errors and marking in margins the same words over and over: *vague, elaborate, wordy,* or my favorite, *AWK.* Once in awhile, a fresh and cleverly written essay pops out of the stack and this teacher sits back to read it, a little smile or even a giggle passes his or her lips, and after reading it, he or she makes a nice big A in the upper-right corner, with one of these words: *Coherent! Cohesive! Cogent! Well-written!*

What a stereotypical and uncomplicated view of the person responsible to teach hordes of young persons to write in an organized, grammatical, and meaningful way. But I know the portrait is not too far removed from reality because at different points of my adulthood, I have been that lonely English teacher; until I met and worked with Lucy Calkins and a group of brilliant writers and educators at Teachers College Reading and Writing Project in New York City, and until I read great books about assessment and response to writing such as Mina Shaughnessy's *Error and Expectations,* and Jane Hansen's *When Writers Read,* I did not realize I had options for how to respond to writing. I hated to witness myself reading and marking papers like that, but what alternative did I have? It was not how the poets, essayists, and novelists in my college writing courses talked and wrote about each other's writing, but it was how my own high school and college essays were graded, so I was simply playing teacher, exactly as I had when I was seven years old, making the kids on my block do homework in my little classroom in our den. My favorite part of this play teaching was checking the spelling quizzes I gave and marking incorrect answers with a big red X. (It's a wonder I had any friends at all in my neighborhood—what a bossy-head I was!)

The problem with my way of marking papers as a salary earning, adult teacher was that the kids who got the "well-written" on their paper felt great. Perhaps they could bank this A away with all the other kudos they've received throughout their years in school. They may not have completely understood what they did to deserve this reward, but so what? It felt great to get one. The kids whose papers radiated red ink, who read my margin comments and looked furtively back and forth from those comments to their writing, completely flummoxed by most of the marginalia, felt defeated and possibly angry—frustrated, at the least.

While we have learned some fine alternatives, such as portfolio collections, self-assessment surveys, and to some extent, rubrics, to the red ink "AWK" in the margin, most of us have a long way to go toward creating assessments that *teach* writing rather than sort, humiliate, and confuse. The kids who have difficulties with conventional language syntax and text structures try so hard to follow directions, to make their writing look and sound like the number 4, exemplary essay on the state writing test, and they often think they have done a pretty good job. But once again, they have missed the cues and failed to conform, and this becomes one more notch in their belts of failure. They will avoid writing in school and as adults because they will always have those red-penned comments and those numerical scores in their heads as they try to compose their thoughts and feelings on paper.

Alternatives for Reading Student Writing

What we need are alternative tools and structures for noticing and naming what our students are doing as writers that take into account writers' strengths and individual gifts and build teaching on those, instead of on deficits. If possible, we should practice that noticing and naming activity with colleagues. Four eyes are better than two, and eight, twelve, twenty eyes can begin to paint a magnificently rich portrait of a young person as a writer, when those eyes are focused on the beauty and brilliance in sample student pieces.

What follows are some suggestions for enacting this powerful work of reading student writing with grade-level colleagues or as a whole-school, whole-faculty pursuit. At the end of the book, I include several blank templates that might prove useful as a way to train the eyes where to look and what to look for. I also suggest places to go for more in-depth information about looking at all kinds of student work, as there are whole books, websites, and education groups devoted to this important cause. Finally, I offer suggestions for structures inside the classroom for students to learn how to look at and talk about each other's work in meaningful and productive ways in writing partnerships and writing groups.

But first, here are some ground rules to keep in mind for how to read student writing, no matter what the occasion and no matter if you are alone or with colleagues:

1. Take time outside of writing workshop to read your students' writing. I used to take ten notebooks or writing folders home every Friday and my Saturday morning ritual involved downing a pot of coffee and delighting in my kids' words. Other teachers grab fifteen minutes during planning periods, at lunch or after school, to spend extra time with one student's writing.

2. Reread student writing exactly as you would a difficult poem or prose text, expecting that meaning exists there, even if you can't grasp it immediately.

3. Respond first as a human being. As these teachers from my summer institute section blessedly reminded our group: Ed Shumley said, "It's just a communication between people. If you think of it like that, you're more apt to respond in a human way." You could say, as Claudia Vecchio did, "Your writing makes me want to respond like a reader—to just put my teacher self aside." Or as Melissa did: "That scar has its own story and you told it." Or as Emily Sobczuk said, "Your writing makes me want to run off and write about my own memories." Or as Cheryl Tyler said, "These words are gentle, just like you."

4. Read with sticky notes on hand, or if using a copy of the original, mark in the margins, underline, circle, and star arresting places. Write encouraging words. These will carry long-lasting weight and will motivate your kids to write more and care about their writing.

5. As often as possible, read and discuss student writing with colleagues. Many eyes make reading easier and more fun.

6. Be ready to be surprised. Be open to laugh, or cry, or feel your heart move, as one human being who has been trusted with the heart and soul of another human being.

> ### Opportunities for Reading Student Writing
>
> - Alone, with only your mind and a pen and sticky notes
> - With an individual student beside you to explain her thinking about her process and her intentions (for much more about conferring into student intentions, see Carl Anderson's *How's It Going?* [2000] and *Assessing Writers* [2005])
> - With a small group of students, again, ready and willing to explain their thinking and intentions
> - With a partner teacher
> - With grade-level teachers, across-grade level or discipline area faculty members and administrators, university researchers, writers

Structures for Reading Student Writing with Colleagues

Partner Teacher

As a great partner or friend can make any life situation more tolerable and easier to handle, a teaching partner, or school friend, can add energy, knowledge, and humor to the art of reading and assessing student writing. We all need at least one like-minded colleague in our school buildings or else we can grow lonely and disparaged about the work of teaching. We begin mumbling to ourselves and wondering, "Am I crazy . . . or is this truly happening?" and a teaching buddy can assure us that yes, it (whatever *it* is) is indeed happening!

Many teachers I know come to crave time to be with their teaching partners to look at kids' work and talk about the teaching of writing. Sometimes teachers share suggestions of how to help struggling writers, but just as often, they ask how to teach the "superstar" writers in the class—you know, the ones for whom clever language and ideas come as easily as breathing. How can we help those writers stretch as well?

Grade-Level, Across-Grade-Level, and Across-Discipline-Area Groups

In many elementary and middle schools I work with, structures are in place for grade-level articulation groups or professional learning communities to meet at least once a month, if not weekly. These groups are quite busy with agenda items concerning all the discipline areas, with data entry for benchmark testing, with requests from administrations and plans for schoolwide celebrations and performances. But still, groups of teachers realize that scheduling time to look at student writing across the year can yield tremendous bounty—from ideas for genre minilessons to specific teaching content for writing conferences. What if these groups made a routine to read and talk about a few pieces of student writing every time they meet?

I want to make a plug here for creating vertical, across-grade-level, even across-discipline-area groups for looking at student work. Music, art, gym, and content-area teachers can offer valuable insights about the learning habits and strengths of our students that make us wonder sometimes if we are talking about the same child. Teachers of language arts and English classes have been amazed at what student writing looks like at different age levels. For one thing, upper-grade teachers are often impressed with the voice, intelligence, and emotional honesty in young kids' work. Primary teachers can see where their students are going—how thinking on the page deepens and fits into ever more complicated structures. They can learn what upper-grade teachers pay attention to, and what they might do to help lay the groundwork for that. Interestingly, teachers of different grade levels can come to discover that they all teach things like commas, paragraphing, and the spelling of *there, their,* and *they're* every single year and still, in twelfth grade, kids struggle with those concepts. We can no longer blame any particular grade level but must come to the conclusion that mastery of some complex language and text features may not come in a given grade or at a certain age, or may come much later in the literacy learning journey.

One last obvious benefit of across-grade collaboration is that when individual kids need specific help with basic skills or with more sophisticated strategies that we feel unprepared to explain, the teachers of older or younger kids might have excellent ideas that can help.

Study Groups

I've been privileged to be a member and also a facilitator of dozens of teacher and administrator study groups. Most of these met in a lovely school library. Other groups met outside of members' schools, in university classrooms, in public libraries, and in members' houses. I know of a group of teachers in Austin, Texas, that meets to talk about curriculum and planning in a coffeeshop every Saturday morning. Often, these groups receive support from school and district administrations, special grants, or local writing projects and networks. In some cases, teachers were paid small stipends to attend, but again, as with the formal and informal partnerships that teachers form inside schools, these study groups felt to their members like lifelines in the rushing current of daily teaching, and they attended without monetary compensation because they wanted to.

I've participated in and led study groups that include members from outside schools. Occasionally, a guest writer might join a meeting and offer insights from his or her professional experience. Some districts take advantage of their proximity to colleges and universities to partner with education professors and their students in study groups or in classes that meet inside schools and use classrooms as learning sites. If your school does not participate in university partnerships, and this idea interests you, please, contact the literacy department at your local college and ask if you could get involved in some kind of study or relationship. Most literacy and language professors I know are eagerly searching for willing teachers and classrooms in which to do research.

Study groups can form around any topic imaginable, some even become book clubs and writing groups for teachers' personal work. I'm focusing this section specifically on groups that organize around reading student writing to offer another option for collaborative work for the ultimate benefit of all students. What follows is an example of what one study group I've participated in looks like.

In Austin, Texas, where I live, some teachers from different schools gather once a month after school to read student writing and to talk about what they see and how to help their students. These teachers are not paid for their time, unfortunately, and they all have to drive some distance to reach the meeting place, but the benefits of their collaboration give them the will and energy to continue meeting. They are all teachers of students who are English language learners (ELLs) in third to eighth grade. These teachers put a piece of student writing on an overhead projector or beneath a document camera so that everyone's eyes can be on the text at once. Then they read it, notice what the student is doing well, and what they might teach next for that individual student.

Some of the teachers are fluent Spanish speakers and others are not. They help each other notice the ways in which their students, mostly Spanish speakers, compose sentences that reflect Spanish grammar and syntax. This is profound work. To look at a sentence written by a young person who is learning a new language, in some cases, the third or fourth language, and to be able to name how that sentence conforms perfectly to Spanish syntax, even though it sounds odd according to English syntax, recognizes and appreciates what that student knows. I remember that the first time someone pointed this out, we all responded with a gasp; our eyes were opened and a new way of reading student writing became possible. A fifth grader named Benito had written this first sentence of his personal narrative about going to Zilker Park in Austin: "At Zilker Park there is a ocean but little water."

As a group, we puzzled over this sentence for several minutes. For one thing, there certainly is not an ocean anywhere in or around Austin, Texas, so that threw us off. Finally, someone noticed that Benito had scribbled in the word *whit* [with], so that the sentence could read: "At Zilker Park there is a ocean with little water." One of the bilingual teachers suddenly blurted out, "Oh! He might mean *lake* or *pond* but not have that word yet. So he's trying to describe a body of water that maybe looks almost as big as an ocean to him, but it has less water!" We all learned that day about how language learners will often use circumlocutions, describe in a roundabout way, when they cannot reach for the word that they want. Benito's teacher, Kristel Nichols, was sensitive enough not to instantly mark this as incorrect, but rather to ask him to say more about the place. We often become overly concerned with the idea that there is exactly one word or phrase to say things. While "an ocean with less water" might be a technically or scientifically incorrect name for a lake or pond (and by the way, the body of water in Zilker Park that Benito refers to is called "Barton Springs," and it looks like and functions as an enormous swimming pool, so it is variously called springs, pool, pond, and lake), his circumlocution works perfectly well in a personal narrative, and in fact is quite a lovely, poetic way to describe this place.

Formalized Protocol for Looking at Student Work

Several ongoing programs and centers provide information, professional development, and paper and online materials for looking at student work. While most of these resources are geared to looking across discipline-area products and processes, most can easily be tweaked to fit writing specifically. What I like about the values and procedures of these different initiatives is that most suggest gathering entire school faculties and communities around a student(s) portfolio of work from every discipline. The purpose is not to evaluate or grade, but to learn who this young person is; what gifts and strengths he or she possesses; what we can do as a *faculty* or *school community* to help him or her fit in and excel.

In the next few pages, I discuss briefly the sources I know of and think are extraordinary for providing guidance and tools for looking at student work in order to benefit all students.

"The Descriptive Review," Patricia F. Carini, author and educator

I have read about Pat Carini's work and watched some demonstrations of the process she devised for systematically looking at students' learning and work. Carini may be one of the biggest influences on the growth and development of the idea of focusing on how students go about learning and making something instead of instantly evaluating and passing judgment on what he or she did. Carini designed something called the "Descriptive Review of the Child," which leans on the knowledge and experience that everyone in the home, school, and community have about a child, so that each child emerges as a complex being with multiple strengths and attitudes. She calls on teachers and families to truly look at and listen to their children, to recognize their moods and gestures, their full selves. Carini's words and ideas are profoundly elegant, beautiful, and important for parents and guardians, and all the adults responsible for the lives of children.

For a presentation of Carini's philosophy and descriptive processes, I suggest reading *From Another Angle: Children's Strengths and School Standards: The Prospect Center's Descriptive Review of the Child*, edited by Margaret Himley, with Patricia Carini (2000). The book includes the extremely detailed stories of the descriptive reviews of three students in primary, fourth grade and high school, with samples of their work and comments from their presenting teachers.

National School Reform Faculty

National School Reform Faculty (NSRF) is a professional development initiative that includes concepts of Facilitative Leadership and Critical Friends Groups (CFG). Critical Friendships are a specific type of learning committee that uses formal protocols to help educators collaborate on improving practice. Located at the Harmony Education Center in Bloomington, Indiana, NSRF offers many resources at its physical location and online (nsrfharmony.org) for schools wishing to form CFGs to help improve teaching practices for the benefit of students. While NSRF provides several formal work review protocols, I also know schools that have modified the NSRF forms to fit their own sites and circumstances. Elaine Bakke, a literacy coach in Livingston, New Jersey, shared with me that they began the school year using the protocol called "ATLAS: Learning from Student Work," available on the NSRF website.

Here is an example of a semiformal process for looking at student writing that I borrowed and modified a bit from one of the protocol resources on the NSRF website:

1. A teacher copies and distributes a collection (preferably) of student work that she wishes to submit to group feedback. Her initial question might be, what do you notice?
2. The teacher removes herself from the conversation, taking notes on what her colleagues say but not commenting until the very end of the process.
3. First round: Teachers respond, pointing out as many positive features as possible.
4. Second round: Teachers suggest teaching points to help the student grow as a writer.
5. Third round: The student's teacher finally responds, filling in background information on the student, asking questions, and deciding to follow through with suggestions.

A variation on this approach might be that the initiating teacher fills in background information about the student first (he or she is an ELL, has repeated a grade, is new to the school), if that needs to be taken into account before teachers begin to comment on the writing.

Looking at Student Work Website

Looking at Student Work (LASW, www.lasw.org) is a fantastic website for links to books, articles, videos, and protocols devoted to the careful and close examination of student work in a variety of contexts and for numerous purposes. According to the Welcome page, LASW is "an association of individuals and educational organizations that focus on looking at student work to strengthen connections between instruction, curriculum, and other aspects of school life to students' learning." The collaborative formed out of a meeting in 1998 hosted by the Chicago Learning Collaborative and The Annenberg Institute for School Reform (which was the parent organization of NSRF).

Strategies for Reading Student Writing

Remember that my impassioned plea in this book is that as teachers of writing, we should give the same amount of time, respect, and attitude of inquiry into the mystery in our students' writing that we would give to a published novel, poem, or feature article. Yes, we notice misspelled words, and absolutely, we trip over sentences that don't flow in conventional, logical patterns. But we have decided to take a different stance: to notice the surprises, the brilliance, and the unique tone and signature style of even the most plain or scrawny or meandering piece of student writing.

Whether you are working alone to read your students' writing over a cup of coffee on Saturday morning, or you are lucky to have found a partner teacher or group of colleagues to read it with you, it will help to have a strategy that works best for you to help read for strength first and areas to teach second.

Using the General Reading Protocol Alongside Student Writing

For a basic and simple approach to reading student writing, many teachers have gainfully applied my general reading protocol (Appendix A) for published texts (as discussed in Chapter 3) to their students' writing. I like this approach because it lays the exact same process on top of both published and student texts, thereby giving us practice and experience in treating them as equals. What I wish to add to the protocol in the context of reading student writing is a suggestion to elect a facilitator of the group who can keep time and conversation flowing. I recommend the facilitator set a timer or watch the clock and allow five to ten minutes for positive comments (for the first three items on the protocol) about student work. From experience, I know this is not so easy to do! I recognize that teachers have zero time in their schedules and they long for help to know what to teach, especially to kids who have difficulties with writing. You will need to trust me here until you witness it for yourselves: time spent looking at student work with positive eyes yields enough teaching content for weeks. Remember that a precise naming of what an individual student is doing well is valuable teaching, and we should continually lay that foundation; otherwise, it will not matter if we have 100 clever teaching points and suggestions in our magnificent minilessons, students who have difficulties will not hear or use them because they do not address individual writers.

As described in Chapter 3, you can place the general reading protocol (Appendix A) beside student writing and practice the same sequence, first finding places you admire or places that remind you of your own feelings and life experiences. You may need to reread all or parts of student writing (alone or with colleagues). If you have a copy of the original, you can underline, write questions in the margins, and prepare to talk with your reading partner or grade-level or faculty group. Share out parts that make you laugh out loud or that pull up grief, or that make you reconsider a long-held notion. Then tell your students about the compliments and positive responses of other adults.

Templates for Looking at Student Writing

Aside from a protocol for helping to keep our focus *positive* first, it can help to have a template that keeps track of all the things we're noticing and thinking as we read student writing. Some teachers have worried that it is too difficult *not* to see grammar, spelling, and punctuation errors, so I've included a box to park those concerns while we continue looking at what students do well in their writing. Many groups of teachers have gamely practiced using some variation of the template in Figures 8–1 (reproducible version in Appendix C for writing from the whole class and Appendix D for individual student writers). Teachers have given me excellent feedback on how they could imagine using the template, and have alerted me to its strengths and gaps, as well as places to revise, and the version printed here reflects all their helpful comments.

Class: _____   Genre or Unit of Study: _____   Date: _____

Research and Name	
Going Well	Questions for Class

Decide	
Writing Areas to Grow	Spelling, Grammar, Punctuation Concerns

Teach	
Next Minilesson *What:* *How:*	In Future

Figure 8–1   *Looking at Whole-Class Writing*

Examples of What Might Go into Template Boxes

What follows is a brief description of what I mean by the labels inside each box of the template and a few examples of things that teachers in my workshop presentations have noticed and named as we looked at student writing together. Taken as a whole, the boxes provide information for the big moves of a writing conference: *Research* what the class/student knows and does well; *name* one or two of those things before you do anything else; *decide* what you feel is most important to address with the class/ student from the boxes in the middle containing items of concern, *teach* one of them now, and save others for future conferences.

1. *Going Well*: This box contains only positive comments. I encourage teachers to push past surface features like paragraphs and subject/verb agreement, and labels from writing rubrics, like *sequenced, organized,* and *detailed* to more descriptive language such as found in Chapters 4 and 5.

Some examples: purposeful repetition; ending is surprising and sad; music in the combined languages of Spanish and English; sounds like a young adult novel; can see the relationship between the father and son; uses anecdotes that teenagers will relate to as support for the facts; intones truth with a voice like the principal/president/Bible; sounds like prose poetry with rap undertones.

2. *Questions for Author*: This box is a place to capture any questions about process or content that might arise as you read a student's text.

    Some examples: What inspired you to write this? How do you envision this piece continuing? How do you imagine this ending connecting to the title and beginning? What kinds of revision have you done? How old is your main character? Who are you arguing with in this essay? What point are you trying to make?

3. *Writing Areas to Grow*: This box might contain both big concepts about writing, as well as items that pertain to a specific text.

    Some examples: reread to revise; increase stamina; figure out what you really want to say; describe what that character is thinking and how his body might feel as he hits the winning home run; practice breaking the lines of this poem several ways for different meanings and rhythms; brainstorm some possible ways to support your big idea or thesis.

4. *Spelling, Grammar, Punctuation Concerns*: I think this box is self-explanatory, and it will contain whatever surface features shout from the page. One group of high school teachers decided to revise *concerns* to *urgencies*. Have at it!

5. *Next Conference*: After you have listed several items in the writing areas to grow and grammar concerns boxes, you can look over them and decide which *one* (perhaps another item if it's easy to tuck in as you talk) to broach in your next conference with the class/student. Do not try to teach everything you listed in those boxes. You'll have this sheet on file, perhaps in a conferring binder, ready to look at again, should you need to remind yourself what else you meant to teach that class/student. Notice I've included a place for you to decide not only *what* to teach, but *how*: explain, demonstrate, look at mentor texts together, send student to another member of the class to see what advice he or she could give.

    Some examples: What—fiction is about growth and change in main character; how—talk about the character changing in class read-aloud book or in student's independent reading book. What—feature articles take on an enthusiastic teaching voice; how—practice out loud with me—tell me two fascinating ideas about electric guitars.

6. *In Future*: Again, this label is self-explanatory, and it can house whatever items from previous boxes that seem worth teaching next or in the near future. It helps if the issues for future teaching are broad, since you may not get to this student for awhile, and she may have moved on to a new genre or part of the writing process completely.

I suggest that we plan once a month to stack all our students' writing and skim through it using the template called Looking at Whole-Class Writing (Figure 8–1 and Appendix C). The stack might consist, at the beginning of the year, of just our students' writer's notebooks. Later, the stack might include drafts of a genre study—short fiction, for instance. Though we can also use the templates to look at final products of a writing unit, be advised that I do *not* mean for these templates to be evaluative. They are not rubrics that direct us to look for specific, particular text features, but rather lead us to notice and name things in our students' writing that might fall outside any rigid genre guidelines or list of conventions. We use the protocols and templates in this book to be *surprised* by brilliance. They can help train our eyes until seeing hidden gems becomes second nature, until we *expect* to see it, and therefore, we do. To help that happen, I suggest also trying the template variations in Figure 8–2 and Appendix E, which can function as a deliberately organized process toward becoming a different reader of student work.

Looking first at the whole-class stack of writing allows us to scan and skim across kids' writing to get the gist or take the temperature of how the majority of students are doing. Afterward, we can focus on individual students using the template Looking at Individual Student Writing (Appendix D).

A Detailed Protocol for Looking at Student Writing

Earlier, I described using a general reading protocol (Appendix A) for looking at student writing. Here, I offer a more detailed protocol (outlined here and included as a reproducible version in Appendix G). This detailed protocol provides an opportunity

Student Name: _____	Date: _____
Unit of Study: _____	

Initial Thoughts (A parking lot for things that immediately occur to you)

Lens: _____ (e.g., voice, structure, specific genre features. Remember to change your stance toward the positive.)

New Language to Name What I See (from ideas in Chapters 4 and 5)

New Directions to Take (What to teach the class as *writers* rather than surface features of the writing.)
1.

2.

3.

Figure 8–2   *Looking at Whole-Class Writing (Variation)*

to read some humorous, surprising, and beautiful bits of writing out loud to the group, an activity that has amazed groups of teachers around the country when they gave themselves over to finding hidden gems in their students' writing. Again, this activity works best if someone will facilitate and keep a careful watch on the clock. The activity can take anywhere from thirty minutes to an hour, depending on how many minutes you give to each item. I suggest *not* to shorten the minutes of the first step spent looking for what students are doing well; this is the hardest part for many of us and it takes time to relax, to read and reread, and to let the kids' delightful voices wash over us. This protocol makes use of the templates in Appendices C and D.

Whole-Class Writing

1. Skim across a batch of student writing from your whole class. It might be everyone's writer's notebooks or writing folders, complete with drafts, or everyone's final pieces, or benchmark assessment pieces.

2. For ten full minutes, look for responses to put *only* into the box labeled "Going Well" found in the template in Figure 8–1 and Appendix C. (For some teachers with generous spirits and/or knowledge of what to call the things they admired, the "Going Well" box was too small!)

3. For five minutes, group members read out loud a line or a sentence or two that they admire from the writing pieces. Do not preface the sentences with explanations or discuss it afterward. There will be time for that in the next steps of the protocol. This part should sound like a choral performance of powerful language, so belt these lines out with full, appreciative voices.

4. For five minutes, share out and discuss items teachers find as they look through the lens of what is going well for their student writers. Make this language public on charts or document camera projections because this helps "grow" what is possible to say for the whole group.

5. For another ten minutes, teachers can work alone or with a partner to fill in the other boxes on the template.

6. For the next ten minutes, teachers can again share out and discuss with the whole group things they are finding to put in the other boxes of the template.

Individual Student Writing

For a longer meeting or to focus directly on one particular student you can repeat the process I just outlined, using the template in Figure 8–3 and Appendix D (Looking at Individual Student Writing). If you are doing this work at a faculty meeting or in a situation where time is quite limited, I suggest you choose just one student. I usually invite teachers to find a student who is a mystery to them, a source of frustration or discouragement because now they will have help from fellow teachers to find beauty in the writing and come up with ways to name it. The frustration need not be that a student has difficulties making paragraphs or enjoys sprinkling in commas every third word, or uses text-messaging abbreviations, but because the student can write circles around all of us and we are at a loss for how to push him or her.

A benefit to looking at student writing with colleagues is that we can help each other develop new language for naming what our students do well, and take the filled-in templates directly back to share with our kids or to use in conferences with individual writers.

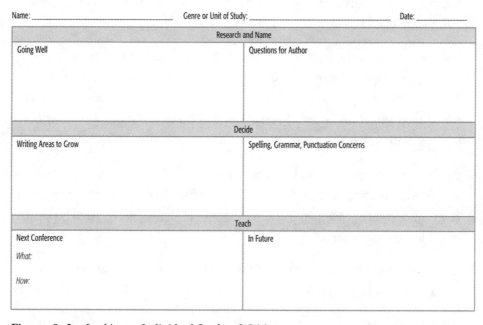

Figure 8–3 *Looking at Individual Student Writing*

Structures for Kids Reading and Talking About Each Other's Writing

Writing Partners

I am the luckiest writer I know because I live in the same house with my writing partner/friend/buddy/husband! Randy and I have written speeches and workshop presentations together, and we co-authored our book, *For a Better World: Reading and Writing for Social Action* (2001). We have a way of working together forged from years of experience that began when we were both doctoral students at Teachers College, Columbia University. When other couples ask us how we can possibly do this, we smile knowingly and answer that at times it wasn't easy, but what we accomplished overall has been rich and meaningful for both of us.

Because we have composed, revised, and published texts together, we have a vivid sense of each other as writers. We know each other's particular strengths and we know areas that always need tweaking. We send each other to book and article resources; we share student writing and stories of classrooms. We respect each other's writing talents and knowledge so much that we are often each other's first reader of any book and article drafts that we send out. We trust each other and follow each other's advice much (though not all) of the time. We know that we can always count on each other to gush over the good spots (I always write "Yummy!" in the margins of Randy's work), and suggest alternative words, phrases, and structures for the places that need work.

Over my history as a writer, I have also had special poetry friends, memoir and fiction readers. Again, in the years I was writing those kinds of texts, I could not imagine doing so without my friends by my side, inspiring me to write better, seeing strengths I didn't know I had, and then offering sound, constructive advice for areas I needed help with. Since I have leaned on my fellow writers so heavily over all the decades I've been a writer, I know how crucial these relationships can be. I want to offer this same inspiring and practical relationship to my students, so that they might feel the power of a writing friend. We want our students to do well, so we have to demonstrate and teach what being a good writing partner means, and then we have to give them time to practice and time to grow into the role of the writing partner. Here are some things to think about and try when introducing and maintaining writing partnerships:

- Invite an actual writing friend to come to your class to talk about how the two of you provide writing help for each other.
- Show a piece of your own writing that received helpful comments written in the margins or in a letter or email, or jot down verbal comments that someone made about your piece. Talk about what you learned, and what you revised as a result of someone's comments.
- In a minilesson, demonstrate with a student volunteer what a "bad" partner looks and sounds like. I have acted out, in a real drama queen way, looking around the room while my partner reads her piece; getting distracted by what someone in the room is doing or saying; and responding with a shrug, a grunt, or an unhelpful, "It's good."
- Introduce the simplified reading protocol in Appendix H for kids to use with their writing partners. Provide time for kids to practice using it.
- Demonstrate how to be a strong, helpful partner across more than one minilesson and come at the idea from different angles. For instance, we can model with our student volunteer how to look at our partner and listen closely; how to notice something we love first, and ask questions like: "What part would you like me to look at/listen to?" "Where are you having difficulties?"

As partnerships are maintained over a length of time, the exploratory, beginner-type questions drop away. The writing partners come to know each other's work. They become braver about admitting difficulties to their friends, such as "I suck at dialogue." They learn how to offer guidance, such as "Did you ever find another anecdote for your feature article?"

Writing Groups

The only thing better than a wonderful writing partner is a whole *group* of writing friends. Most writers I know have belonged to a writing group at one time or another. Groups range from extremely formal types, with applications for membership and strict rules for conducting business, to very casual get-togethers to offer cheerleading and companionship, gourmet food, and often, wine! Finding the right group can be, in the outside world, a matter of trial and error. Beginning in college, I have belonged to several writing groups. Typically, we were all serious writers, wanting and needing critical eyes on our work because we all wanted to be published. There were plenty of big egos in every group, and there was often an undercurrent of competition. Our comments could sometimes seem rather cruel, and at least once, I cried over someone's insensitivity. We acted that way because we had not been taught differently! At this stage in my life, I long for more openhearted support in a writing group. I still need critical and educated eyes on my writing, but I want it to come with a good dollop of warmth, kindness, and especially, humor. As traveling for work keeps me away from home a lot, I've tried an online writing group, but nothing substitutes for the gasps, laughter, tears, and cheers of a live audience for writing.

Lucky kids in our classrooms. They don't have to go searching the classifieds or the Internet for local writing groups. They don't have to drive any distances to get to the meeting, and they don't have to worry about time or travel schedules. All our students have to do is practice and learn how to be strong, supportive group members.

I teach students how to be in writing groups by following the same ideas I listed for teaching about partnerships. Once the groups are in motion and I find some predictable social and organizational obstacles as I confer with them, I lean more heavily on the kids to watch and learn from each other. I ask for a volunteer group to carry on a conversation in front of the other students (sometimes called a "fishbowl" conversation), where the classroom audience forms a circle around the demonstration group and observes everything from how the group begins, how they take turns, ask each other clarifying questions, offer positive, collegial advice and suggestions, and so on.

Teachers often wonder how kids will know what to say about each other's writing, beyond "I like the part," or "where did you get the idea to write this?" I suggest that you wait to form writing groups until after kids have been with you for a few months and have developed some language about writing from your minilessons and conferences. Writing group members might also use Appendix H for their response group work and practice responding first to what they admire and what moves them and then naming it with language that resonates for them.

After my Teachers College summer institute participants took our field trip to find great language on the backs of books at the Columbia University bookstore (see Chapter 5), Roxanna Lopez thought her kids could also go on a field trip, or a "language treasure hunt" to the school library. Danielle Howard imagined making a bulletin board full of elevated phrases from book blurbs to immerse her students in the language of specific compliments to give their partners and groups that build up confidence while also pointing out qualities their friends might not have been aware of in their own writing.

Finally, I teach kids directly, all year long, to keep running lists of questions to bring to a writing conference with me, to a partnership, or to a peer group, and to come prepared with writing puzzles they need help solving or small sections they would like to read out loud to an audience to get feedback.

How Administrators, Literacy Coaches, and Instructional Leaders Can Help Support This Work

Devoted and passionate teachers will always find the time, place, and resources to do the work they believe will help their students whether or not they are provided these things. However, such teachers end up feeling frustrated and exhausted when they have to proceed without administrator support, and research shows that these talented and dedicated teachers leave the classroom in droves. Administrators can stem the bleeding tide of great teachers by providing physical and emotional support for their important work that will reap benefits beyond any one-day professional development or any binder full of assessment materials. Here are some ideas for carving time and space for teachers to gather together to look at student writing. In every situation, of course, the work will improve dramatically if instructional leaders, coaches, principals, and department chairs are present and working alongside classroom teachers. In school buildings where administrators carve out time to visit classrooms to talk with students about their literacy learning, not as supervisors making judgments, but as adults who also read and write, kids make remarkable progress in their literacy learning and their general motivation and well-being in school. Here are several suggestions for supporting faculty members working collaboratively to help improve teaching practice and student learning:

- Provide time for teachers to have grade-level meetings and study groups around reading student writing. Study groups should be interest- and topic-driven. They might meet only once a month (dates and times should be prearranged and remain unchanged) and last no longer than two hours. A facilitator can gather consensus about what to study, what research and data collection to perform in classrooms, and what and how much to read (an article, a single chapter in a professional book) before the next scheduled meeting.

- Set up a several weeks-long course with noticing and naming what their students know as writers as the central topic. Jen Jeffries, an inventive literacy coach at PS 172, Brooklyn, New York, invited teachers to each bring the work of one student to the meeting, and get help naming the writing strengths of that student from all the positive eyes around the table. Then teachers practiced saying those positive things to the student over the following weeks, and brought the stories and new sample writing to the next meeting to relate how it went and to look for signs of growth in the new writing pieces.

- Support teachers and coaches attending professional workshops and conferences. Every professional person spends some amount of her work life continuing to learn about her craft and profession. Brain surgeons attend technology classes; pilots renew their licenses. Teachers and coaches must also pursue continuing education in current issues, research, and methodologies for teaching in the twenty-first century. Administrators are often the sole means of support for teachers wishing to increase their knowledge.

- Attend and participate in all professional development that you might provide for teachers and coaches. This sends a message of what is valued to all in the building, and it also allows you to understand what to expect to see and hear in writing classrooms.

- Turn the focus of this book from student writing to looking with new lenses at the beauty and brilliance in teachers' work. Look at growth, risk taking, collaborating, leadership, and most important, a willingness to continue learning. Look for an individual's particular gifts: management, organization of time and even of paperwork (trust me, that is a talent), calm tone, student/teacher trust, powerful math, science, social studies/history teaching, contributions to the profession through writing articles or blogs, and presenting at workshops and conferences.

If we want to change the conversation in schools about how we can read student writing in ways that celebrate their strengths and motivate them to revise and keep writing, we will need to do that work with our colleagues. It will not help if one lone teacher in one grade level operates from a curriculum of strength and names powerful writing identities for her students, and then when those students proceed to the next grade level, someone responds to their work only by circling errors in red pen. This work of shifting how we read and respond to student writing should permeate entire school buildings, entire school systems, and that will only happen if we do it together.

How Do We Think Through Official Evaluation and Grading as Response to Student Work?

Ironically, grades and tests, punishments and rewards are the enemies of safety;
they therefore reduce the probability that students will speak up and that truly
productive evaluation can take place.
—ALFIE KOHN

I'm trained to look for their needs—how can I meet their needs?
It's such a flip to look at strengths and teach from there.
—JEN JEFFRIES, PS 172

This book focuses on responding to student writing, noticing and naming what each and every student does brilliantly and beautifully in writing, with language that writers and craftspersons of all kinds use to articulate their processes and their intentions. I argue that in this precise and educated naming, we not only bolster the writing identities of our young students, so that they might say, *I am one who writes*, but also *teach* them something powerful about writing: how to reach a reader. This moment of truly noticing and naming for an individual what he or she can already make has more potential for student learning, I believe, than the most succinct minilesson or erudite lecture about the qualities of good writing. And its power for motivating writers to want to write more and to make what they write even better surpasses any grading or evaluation system ever devised. This moment of naming is like a spotlight, an insight, a reflection, a blessing. It is not judgmental. It names what is and how perfectly that works for now. It is enough.

How oddly difficult for most of us to accept in our competitive, goal-oriented, Westernized culture, to believe that saying something is *enough* might actually be the most profoundly motivating word for a student to hear. Most of us were raised to think that we could never be enough, and that we must continually strive to do better, be better. Schools have helped ensure that we would never stop our earnest endeavors by devising letter grades as tokens of achievement or failure on assorted tasks and tests of knowledge. A teacher's job inside this system of rewards and punishments is to judge who is eligible for the prize of an A, and who must suffice with lower grades, and occasionally, who must fail. No teacher enjoys this aspect of an otherwise satisfying career, but most acquiesce because grades are the coin of the realm, the market economy in schools, so teachers, students and parents come to believe that it is all of our jobs to supply that economy.

Grades sort and classify who is the best and the brightest, and they dangle like carrots or swords, depending on how easy and comfortable it is for individuals to fulfill the tasks and expectations that result in a grade. For many learners who have difficulty meeting those criteria, grades and increasingly, test scores, come to define who they are and map the course of their lives in everything from career choice to interpersonal relationships. (Have you ever lived with someone who considers himself or herself a bad or a nonreader because of receiving low grades in school? It makes daily living a kind of nightmare for everyone involved.)

When it comes to the discipline of writing, grades create utter chaos for students and teachers. Teachers must contend with the mixed messages they send, calling writing a process, accepting students' slow and occasionally backward movement as they grapple with ever-increasing abstractions in composition and grammar. Chris Anson calls this "the schizophrenia of roles—now the helpful facilitator, hovering next to the writer to lend guidance and support, and now the authority, passing critical judgment on the writer's work; at one moment the intellectual peer, giving feedback, and at the next the imposer of criteria, the gatekeeper of textual standards" (1989, 2). Unfairly, students are not allowed to return the favor of rating our writing with grades or number scores. For students, grades turn learning how to write into a kind of trial or into a competition, which tends to freeze the thought processes and creativity of all but the most hardy of humans. I can only theorize the reasons why, but letter grades atop pieces of writing often feel highly personal to writers, whether the grade is an A or a C. Writing, more than any other activity in school, requires intense thinking and feeling translated into logical organization, lovely language, and persuasive rhetoric. When we tally up spelling and grammar errors, or bleed red ink all over students' writing in the form of corrective marginal comments, we send a subliminal message that kids' very thinking is incorrect, their actual memories, their sense of the world, their interests and passions are not good enough. It doesn't help to mark an A on top either; for students who are used to seeing that, making anything less, even an A– can crush the heart and create confusion that usually takes the form of "What is wrong with me?"

Thinking Through Differences in Assessment and Evaluation

Before I proceed with this exploration of grading and evaluation as response to student writing, I think it useful to make some distinctions between evaluation, or grading, and assessment. Assessment has different meanings to different interested "clients" as David Pearson calls them (Brenner, Pearson, and Reif 2007, 261), and I have my own as well. While I abhor grading in general, and applied to writing specifically, I *love* assessment and believe that we must assess our students' learning of writing frequently and in as much detail as we can muster, and we must continually report what we find to students, families, communities, and school administrations. I believe that *assessment* describes the practices that all teachers engage in, all day long, and it is what must drive our teaching. When I saw my fifth-grade students waiting in the cafeteria before school started, I assessed that some had not gotten enough sleep the night before, and for a few, I knew it was because they were watching *World Wide Wrestling* past midnight. When my students entered class, I ascertained from their body language and energy level whether they had eaten breakfast that morning. If not, I offered fruit or sent them back to the cafeteria for some milk and cereal.

All day long, teachers "take the temperature" of their students' emotional, physical, and behavioral conditions. We can tell from their body language and facial expressions, as well as their outright verbal comments, whether they are grasping the concepts and explanations from our lessons. We take rapid mental and written

> We make thousands of decisions per minute, like the wings of hummingbirds beating incessantly.

notes to call a parent or guardian or talk with the school psychologist about a student who concerns us. We make thousands of decisions per minute, like the wings of hummingbirds beating incessantly, whether to reteach a concept, how long to extend work on a task or assignment, how to organize the social configurations for each activity, when to ease up and when to clamp down—all without benefit of checklists, report cards, grades, or scores. We must assess or we cannot teach. The student-teacher relationship is a constant dance, and without watching, listening, and making some kinds of decisions based on what we see and hear, we cannot know what our next step should be.

Evaluation is the country to which everything that carries weight and value in schools always moves. I don't like this land because it bores and scares me (for all the reasons listed in Chapter 2), but I know this is the country where teachers and schools live. *Evaluation* involves measuring some criteria and placing a numerical or letter grade value on it. In the last twenty years, I've witnessed more streamlined and standardized approaches to deciding what to value and how much it counts. Math, science, and even social sciences seem easy enough to find categories and specific bits to measure, but still, as everyone knows, writing slips away from our best attempts to quantify it.

Grading and test scores, unlike the constant observing and adjusting of teaching and learning that assessment affords, attempt to take the measure of a learner's performance over brief periods of time, and on limited items, and make judgments about the success or failure on that specified task, usually in comparison with other students' performances. Grading attempts to be objective, like a thermometer measuring a fever, but anyone who has tried to assign a letter grade to a poem knows that in many areas of the curriculum, grading can be nothing but subjective.

For generations, kids in school have received letter grades or numbers (which kids and their parents translate immediately into letter grades, no matter how cleverly we recast our evaluation systems) to describe who they are as learners. Grades and scores carry tremendous power in kids' lives: they can earn money, video games, computers, or they can send kids to detention or render them housebound until they improve; they can pave the way into prestigious schools, or they can cause schools to hold kids back and repeat a grade, with kids who are younger and shorter and not their friends.

But Don't Students Need Grades in Order to Improve Their Writing?

I have taken and will continue to take the stance that writing should not be graded. In order to believe that, all we have to do is imagine ourselves as adults in a professional development workshop in our districts, turning in a piece of writing to the presenter, especially the type of writing we often ask our students to do—significant, personal, exploratory, revelatory—and receive a grade of A, B, or, unimaginably, an F. We would simply rebel. We would not attend that PD workshop. We might never write again!

When I present to upper-grade teachers, they inevitably ask about grading, rubrics, and tests, again because this is the world we are living in right now. (I do not address writing tests in this book, but for ideas for preparing students by teaching memoir and personal narrative writing, see Chapter 9 in my book, *Writing a Life* [2005].) Teachers wonder how students will ever learn to write conventionally if we are not continuously correcting their errors. But the truth is that constant correcting and performing for a final grade "freezes student work" (Huot 2002, 73). Grades create competitive, nervous, and perfectionist monsters out of the A students, and bored, rebellious, writing-haters out of the C and below students. Grades have self-fulfilling prophecy tendencies and I believe that they basically bring a halt to learning. Learning requires risk taking, and students who are used to making As do not risk *not* making As. Students with lower grades do not risk being even *more* wrong. Most important, grades lie. Robert Probst writes: "The problem is not simply that the grade doesn't inform; rather, it misinforms and deceives. It imitates the precision of mathematics, though it is at best only impression and judgment. In so doing it conceals information that might be useful to students and parents, and trains them to accept an empty symbol as surrogate" (1988, 224).

Probably as long as evaluation of students has existed, writing instructors have cautioned that students learn to write by writing and not from having their errors hunted down and or being judged by a grade. Steven Zemelman and Harvey Daniels, early in their wonderful book, *A Community of Writers: Teaching Writing in the Junior and Senior High School*, quote the Roman rhetorician Marcus Fabius Quintillian, who advised writing teachers of 91 AD that "Youthful minds sometimes give way beneath the weight of correction excessively severe, become despondent and grieve and in the end . . . in their fear of blundering everywhere, attempt nothing" (1988, 13).

Quintillian encouraged "boldness" and "exuberance" over correctness. And school systems have been ignoring him ever since.

People don't learn to do anything well when what they are learning is being scrutinized and evaluated as good or bad, right or wrong. As Zemelman and Daniels point out, "In real life we rely very little on external evaluation and much more on practice—unmonitored, unsupervised, uncriticized practice—as the key way of learning almost everything important: talking, walking, relating to others, riding a bicycle, playing an instrument" (209).

Do Rubrics Make Evaluation Fair?

Rubrics, those descriptive grids and templates, and checklists of criteria have introduced the possibility for a more just method of evaluating kids. Rubrics allow teachers to explain, in more precise detail, not only what is expected in terms of content, form, and appearance of an assignment (the goals), but also what those goals will look like if they are exemplary or if they are poor. Supposedly, all students have to do is follow the rubric like a map. If they want to get an A or a 4 on a piece of writing, they know to do this, this, and this, and it should match the requirements for a score of 4.

Unfortunately, rubrics and checklists can only measure according to the specific language that fits on the lines of a checklist or inside boxes of a grid. They limit and circumscribe according to what one teacher or one group of evaluators believes is important to know. Vicki Spandel cautions that well-meaning rubrics that set out to assess what matters in writing end up assigning points to what is most obvious, what is easy to see, such as "neatness, choice of topic, use of a pen rather than a pencil, perceived effort, length, or close adherence to the assignment" (2001, 6).

Most alarmingly, rubrics can tend toward standardization of writing quality; the descriptors determine outcomes, not allowing for innovation, inspiration, or individualization. Teachers who must adhere strictly to mandated evaluation guidelines and rubrics end up developing lesson plans and crafting their writing feedback to ensure that students will deliver according to evaluation criteria. Students who relish following instructions and making the highest scores possible will study the high end of a grading continuum and perform exactly to those criteria, avoiding growth and risk taking in their writing because it might result in a lower score.

When Randy and I bought a car several years ago, we were energetically encouraged to participate in an "evaluation enterprise" of the local dealership for the parent corporation. There was a short list of survey questions for determining if service had been excellent, good, fair, or poor. The questions were about behaviors and issues the corporate overseers deemed important to conducting their business, so, for example, we were asked: "Were you greeted at the door?" This is a yes or no question! How do you answer "excellent, good, fair, or poor" to that? We were greeted "poor"? In truth, we were not greeted at all; we spent a good thirty minutes wandering around outside in the show lot, opening and closing car doors and inspecting the price sticker on windows. The dealership was exceedingly busy that day, and no one spoke to us until we were standing beside someone's desk inside.

Another question: "Did our sales partner explore financial options?" we wanted to write in: "Yeah, about 11 million times!" We did have a few complaints about the sales service, but none of the items on the checklist matched our concerns. The salesperson did precisely what he was supposed to do according to the rubric: nothing more, nothing less. So we ignored the whole "evaluation enterprise," which is precisely the response that many hard-working and dedicated teachers have toward the use of rubrics, especially in literacy learning. Perhaps evaluations and rubrics help businesses know how to better satisfy clients and thereby reap profits from them. Perhaps trending and number-crunching work in corporate climates will reveal areas of low and high profitability. Certainly standardization is called for when manufacturing hazardous machine parts. Those practices, when applied to pieces of student writing, just seem limiting at best and harmful for burgeoning writers at worst.

In many schools and districts in our nation, rubrics have been crafted by external bodies: district personnel, who may or may not have been classroom teachers; consultants; and employees of corporations that conveniently (and profitably) write the test, the test preparation materials, and the scoring instruments and sell their tidily packaged materials to school districts. These rubrics become the voice of authority over what, when, and sometimes how teachers teach. Copies are available on district websites and sent home to families in newsletters. Some companies offer preprinted rubrics on glossy cardboard posters, and these seem to take root and propagate on classroom walls and halls of school buildings. Again, while rubrics represent criteria and goals of any reasonable literacy curriculum, they tend to form tight walls around any student who might not fit the descriptors or who might wish to extend *beyond* the prescribed boundaries of the grid. Rubrics, which often assign numbers to describe work that is low performing to exemplary, can cause every bit as much damage as grades do to young persons attempting to find reasons to write in school.

An amazingly brave eighth-grade special education teacher in one of my writing institute courses told me a bit of a rubric horror story. "The eighth-grade bulletin board story is one of the saddest stories in my teaching career," she said. "The assistant principal told us that we could only hang up level 3 or 4 [the highest] on the bulletin boards. I don't know if this was her rule or if it was the rule of the region. I did not have any level 3 or 4 student writing so I decided to hang up my students' work anyway or I would have a blank bulletin board! After all the English teachers' bulletin boards were up, the assistant principal decided to give out awards to teachers for their bulletin boards. I did not receive an award."

A coach in the department stood up for this teacher to the administration, explaining that she and her students had worked as hard as everyone and also deserved an award, but the teacher was adamant: "I told the English coach I did not care about getting an award for a bulletin board. I only care that my students know that I know that they tried their best and I hang their work on the bulletin board to acknowledge their best work. My students look to me for positive reinforcement about the work they are doing in my classroom and hanging their work on the bulletin board is one of the ways I say good job." I truly felt for this teacher and I applaud her courage. She had to improvise in this situation; she was being positioned to treat her children poorly, and she simply could not do it and live with it.

But Still, What About Rubrics, Grades, and Tests?

Since teachers usually must assign grades, and since it doesn't look as if standardized testing is going anywhere but more often and more intense, I want to offer some words of advice for the "reality" or "real world" that teachers remind me they live with every day. The problem with the idea of a "real world" is, it depends. What grade level are you teaching? What kind of school do you teach in? What does your administration expect, and what do the people who care about the kids hope for? The problem with grades is they shut down inquiry and deep conversation about quality, which is too important to just let go of. I present this section about grades with the hopes that someone, somewhere might have access to an "ideal world," and then what to do if you do not.

Part One: The Ideal World

In my ideal world, students would write and publish as often as possible throughout the school year. Writing for others to read and/or hear is the prime motivator for revising and improving one's writing (see more about this in Chapter 10). Students would create writing portfolios that house a collection of works to be assessed, not just a single product, and include examples from a wide variety of genre. Students would select the pieces for portfolio presentation to flesh out a portrait of himself or herself as a writer at this point in time. For each piece of writing, I would ask kids to include artifacts from the entire arc of a piece of writing: notebook entries and drafts showing revisions. Students would write informal essays that describe what he or she learned about writing during the entire process of each selected piece. The writing portfolio would not be a controlling device, but rather a place for students to self-monitor, self-assess, and self-teach. "Our students' folders tell a story," notes the wise and wonderful Deb Johnson, literacy coach at Bay Elementary in Clear Creek School District, Texas. If we present the idea of the portfolio being their story or their memoir of writing to our students, we can ask them questions such as: What story do you want your writing to tell? What was the most exciting change you made as a writer this year? When did writing feel difficult? What else do you want to try as a writer to build up your portfolio?

Reading students' reflections as well as artifacts from their process and finished pieces "alters [teachers] roles within the classroom," notes Brian Huot, and makes them "more responsive and editorial and less judgmental and adversarial" (2002, 73). Imagine how joyful this practice could be if we didn't have to also bend ourselves into pretzels to assign a grade or a score to those collections of work, but rather read them in order to talk with the authors and their families about their strengths and their hopes for what to learn how to do next.

I would conduct family conferences, requesting students to lead the conference and family members to ask questions and make plans to help their child grow as a writer. When discussing with parents how their child is finding his or her way as a writer, I often lean on a conceptual model created by Mayher, Lester, and Pradl (1983) who state that learning language follows a development course from "fluency to clarity, to correctness." Writing begins in meaning-making, and until students feel "fluent," that is, comfortable, strong, and at ease with putting their thoughts on paper, they cannot work well on the quality of their writing; they cannot move toward "clarity" (organization, logical sentence flow) or "correctness" (grammar and punctuation). In the version of the fluency to correctness continuum that I use with students and parents, I changed "correctness" to "conventionality" because *correct* implies some kind of permanent, bound-by-law language system, when rules are genre, culture, and time-bound, according to social conventions, and they change (as I discussed in Chapter 2). This fluency to conventionality continuum helps me describe where students operate at a certain point in time.

Part Two: The "Real" World

I put "real" in quotes because reality is slippery. But if we must grade, then we should do so thoughtfully, aiming to minimize the damage that grades can have on our students. Until noticing the hidden gems in our students' writing becomes second nature, we have to find ways to counteract the wave of negativity most of us feel when looking at student writing so that we don't fall instantly into the mire of counting errors and assigning percentages. We have to force ourselves, by whatever means possible, to see intelligence and beauty first and foremost. Then, rather than rush to correct or grade the weaker aspects of a student's writing, we must first grant agency to the writer and be curious enough in our conferences to ask: What work have you done to help clarify meaning for me and your other readers? If a student has indeed sorted out a sentence puzzle or rearranged sections to achieve a more sensible flow of information, we should ask: How did you figure that out? The writer will become more independent in this process, and will begin to articulate her process, intentions, and her writing problems, ultimately becoming her own best editor, rather than a passive receptacle for some authoritative mark or score.

One decent form of assessment that I've seen traveling through schools has teachers writing three "pluses" and one "wish" about students' progress. Such a template that forces us to say more positive than negative, that notes what kids can do instead of what they can't, is called for. This same format could be applied to the writing conference or to written comments on student papers. Donald A. Daiker (1989) writes that sometimes, in order to assess writing more holistically, we just need a "gimmick." He writes, "My own method is to allow myself nothing but positive comments during an initial reading of a student paper; I lift my pen to write words of praise only" (107). I love the almost Biblical sound of that: "I lift my pen to write words of praise only" could be a mantra in our heads or a banner above our desks to remind us to look with positive eyes at our students' writing.

And then, if I still had to assign letter grades in writing, let's say to a group of eighth graders, the first thing I would do is begin a conversation with administration and colleagues about possible alternatives to grading writing. I would never accept one method for all time, but rather continue to argue, question, read resources (see the end of the chapter for a few good books to use to begin a faculty-wide conversation about assessment), and revise the system. Next, if a grade for writing (or a lump grade for language arts, in many schools) must be submitted, I would enlist students' help with their own grades. I would talk through a list of "wishes, hopes, and dreams" for their writing processes and content learning, perhaps something like the list of qualities in Chapter 4, and ask them to compare my list to their portfolio and then write a short reflective essay or a letter to me, arguing for the grade they would assign themselves. I would make it clear that my checklist is a starting point, not a descriptor of exemplary writing, that this is the least I expect from them, and that what I really want to know is how their writing bends and transforms the list.

I would never grade, and in fact, never make a mark of any kind, positive or negative on the individual entries inside my students' writer's notebooks. I might look at these large categories for notebook expectations, suggested by Randy Bomer: volume, variety, thoughtfulness (1995, 60–61) and, only if it became necessary, something about appearance or presentation. With students' input, we would craft a rubric from these large categories, and describe as specifically as possible what an accomplished notebook looks like when a writer makes frequent entries, tries different kinds of writing and explores numerous topics, and uses the page to think about the world. I would assign some amount of points to each category so that they would total to perhaps 30 percent of a unit grade.

After allotting some percent to the writer's notebook, I would divide the remaining percent into observable features of a unit of study in writing. Whatever items I list in these categories must be part of the teaching and reteaching I do in minilessons and conferences during the unit of study. I would keep the items to be evaluated simple and somewhat open-ended, like "Tries three large revision strategies before final draft." There must be room in any rubric or checklist for a Nikki Grimes, an e.e. cummings, a Dave Eggers, or a slam poet, so if I create too much specificity, requiring that everyone use a metaphor or simile, for instance, then I have not opened myself to beauty and brilliance I didn't even know was possible. (One of my favorite poems, for instance, called "Poem" by Langston Hughes, is about a friend going away. It contains only twenty-five words, and there is not a single metaphor. Hughes' few, simple words speak volumes about the loneliness of being separated from a best friend, and my throat catches every time I read it.) Instead, I would grade holistically, allowing myself to be intentionally vague because I believe so heartily that I cannot boil a piece of writing down to individual, predetermined traits.

In a pinch, if I had to assign grades in writing, you might catch me making a little list of heavily taught items like line breaks, image, white space, alliteration, or assonance during a poetry study into a quiz for ten points. As long as I keep those grades off of the actual poems my kids write, I am all for creative ideas for collecting grade points!

At least, this is what I think I would do, if pushed against a wall and forced to grade writing. The minute I try to make sense of any grading system, a thousand ifs, ands, and buts arise. When I had to grade kids' writing as a classroom teacher, I suffered the worst cases of procrastination of my life. I felt guilty, insecure, and outraged. Did I make grades up based on nothing but my *sense* of how a student is doing? Yes. Did I change a grade so that some squeaky-wheel student or parent would stop making my life a living hell? Yes. Did I consider brandishing a bad grade like a sword over a student who seemed to care less about anything I was teaching her? I'm afraid I might have. And I don't think I am alone in these responses.

I do not have the answer for how to grade writing. My dream is that this book will help you make the conversations about writing quality with students, parents, teachers, or colleagues, more open-ended and meaningful. When it comes to the practicality of grading, teachers ultimately have to do what makes sense in their particular political and social situations, and try not to let grades and test scores be end points or take the conversation away from working on the quality of writing.

Though it is true that the "reality" in schools makes it appear that grades and tests reign, perhaps we can become courageous enough to know that reality is only what we say it is. Perhaps we can create a different reality by publishing and celebrating writing as often as possible, showing the world how much our students learn and grow as writers when we teach from inside their particular gifts and strengths.

A Few Resources for Opening Faculty Discussions About Grading and Evaluating

ANDERSON, C. 2005. *Assessing Writers.* Portsmouth, NH: Heinemann.

ANSON, C. 1989. *Writing and Response: Theory, Practice, and Research.* Urbana, IL: National Council of Teachers of English.

KOHN, A. 1993. *Punished by Rewards: The Trouble with Gold Stars, Incentive Plans, A's, Praise, and Other Bribes.* Boston: Houghton Mifflin.

PORTER, C., AND J. CLELAND. 1994. *The Portfolio as a Learning Strategy.* Portsmouth, NH: Boynton/Cook.

TCHUDI, S., ed. 1997. *Alternatives to Grading Student Writing.* Urbana, IL: National Council of Teachers of English.

WILSON, M. 2006. *Rethinking Rubrics in Writing Assessment.* Portsmouth, NH: Heinemann.

10

How Can Teachers Become *In Charge of Celebrations* as We Revalue Student Writing?

Last year I gave myself one hundred and eight celebrations—besides the ones that they close school for. I cannot get by with only a few.

—BYRD BAYLOR, *I'm in Charge of Celebrations*

My intention in this book has been to celebrate student writing. I wanted this book to be about finding the beauty and brilliance in every student's work, every day, at every point in the process, in every piece of writing from a simple notebook entry, to a first draft, to a revised and polished version. To celebrate even the struggles and disappointments. To shine a light on the tiniest found moments of joy, the way Byrd Baylor talks about celebrating the way wind passes through mesquite branches. The way joy sometimes whispers, rather than shouts.

I wanted to hold up the sparest, most inelegant, illegible pieces of student writing and say, "Look at this! Look at the fresh, original way this young person spoke of loss; the way this piece about bodily functions made a group of teachers laugh and laugh." I wanted to teach how to see jewels in all students' writing, no matter what difficulties with language use they might exhibit.

As literacy educators, as the people who introduce the power of the written word to young people, we are in charge of the celebrations we pay attention to in our classrooms, with the 25, 40, or 180 young persons in our care. With our words and gestures, we can honor and mark the occasions for writing, and we can help students feel that writing is a right that belongs to everyone, not a mysterious gift for the few—that every person brings his and her personal way of noticing and naming the world.

But sadly, celebration is what we have lost in our current rush of school days. At the beginning of every school year, when we plan our yearlong writing curriculum, we optimistically pencil in (or even commit to multicolored pens!) the starting and ending dates of each unit of study or genre study in writing. We cross out the holidays, inservice staff development days, parent–teacher conference days, and the testing weeks, and what we have left are a few days we can devote to crafting pieces of writing. We mark all the "day 1s" for the exciting beginnings of each unit of study, and we figure out the final days of each unit, the aptly named "celebration days," sometimes even sketching in some balloons or a row of exclamation marks, as if we are just so excited about these days over all the others on our school calendars.

And then school begins. Real children with needs and challenges sit at tables and desks in our classrooms. Real things happen, like flu season that wipes out half the class for a few days, snow days, and unexpected (once my school had a surprise, thankfully delightful or I would have been really mad, Mariachi Band appear on stage) student assembly days. Real administrators impose their own responsibilities for days devoted to assessments and benchmarks, and districts lay on top of all of us their own urgent necessities for curricular and assessment activities. Over all of that hang the standardized tests imposed on every state in the country thanks to the No Child Left Behind Act of 2002, that insists by the year 2014, all children will be 100 percent proficient in all academic subjects.

Somewhere in all these acts of nature and of federal law, those cheerful celebration days get lost. We comment on student papers; we mark grades in our grade books; perhaps we manage to hang writing on a bulletin board when it is finished and edited for correct punctuation, grammar, or spelling, and that becomes the best we can muster for our publication party.

Unfortunately, when writing celebrations get lost, we have lost the number one motivation for writing. For most writers, the reason to write is to have an image of someone at the other end reading (or listening to) your words and ideas, and preferably loving them of course!

> The reason to write is to have an image of someone at the other end reading.

Science fiction novelist Ray Bradbury asks, "What is the greatest reward a writer can have? Isn't it that day when someone rushes up to you, his face bursting with honesty, his eyes afire with admiration and cries, 'That new story of yours was fine, really wonderful!'" (1990, 128). As a writer, I can attest: it's not the only reward I get from working with words, but it surely is the best.

As a writing teacher, I walk a fine line here because I don't want to paralyze writers by forcing them to share, when most people over the age of six already feel worried about being judged. So the job of any writing community is to generate generosity toward each other. An acceptance of all students' attempts at writing must be built into the process from the very start, or else learning how to write feels sterile, scary, and without purpose other than because it's school.

Now, by focusing this last chapter on celebrating and publishing, I may seem to be arguing with my own fiercely held belief in writing as a journey of thought; that when you write, you don't know where you're going until you get there; that the process is messy and recursive and as Donald Murray reminds us, that you write to find out what you didn't know that you knew.

I still believe in all that. Fiercely.

But I think we should know that when we set aside the time and try different ways to respond to and celebrate kids' writing, we are creating better writers. All writers need a *vision* of what's possible to accomplish with writing, that we can make readers laugh and cry, want to learn things, want to change the world, so that we know why we are headed down this long and winding road of drafting, revising, and editing. We need to *experience* having someone outside of our own little heads reading or listening to our writing so that we know how great that feels—the skin chills and heart-pounding thrill of it—so that we will want to repeat those sensations.

It's like piano lessons: consider the difference if, on your first day at the piano teacher's house, all you do is memorize the names of the piano keys and practice some scales (*Woo-hoo*! Can't wait to come back next week and do some more of that!), rather than trying out a fun, real piece of music right away, helping you to hear and imagine what is possible, the emotional pull of music. It's like when you're working on a thousand-piece puzzle or building a model car, boat, or airplane—you need the completed picture on the top of the box to envision what this pile of little pieces and parts will ultimately become.

Frankly, we need to imagine what's possible at the end of writing work because we need a purpose, other than "because it's school," or "because we're practicing for a state test," to write. Having readers that respond to our writing can give us that purpose. Making a text, whether it's a poem, feature article, blog, or tweet, requires envisioning for whom you're writing, even if it's a total stranger, an *invisible other*, and to imagine how the other will respond. You have to visualize your reader curled up in a favorite stuffed chair in the den, or at a desk staring into the blue light of a computer screen, or lying on a towel at the beach, or in row ten of an auditorium.

The poet Billy Collins has a poem about his all-important readers in every book that he has published. As many writers do, he claims that he reads out loud as he is writing because he cannot *process* unless he thinks someone on the other end is accepting it (Yagoda 2004, 99). That's a powerful claim! He is not able to process his thinking and writing unless he feels accepted by the invisible other. Children's book author, Mem Fox says, "Whenever I write, whether I'm writing a picture book, an entry in my journal, a course handbook for students, or notes for the milkman, there's always someone on the other side, if you like, who sits invisibly watching me write, waiting to read what I've written" (1993, 9).

Writing Celebrations Make Powerful Responses to Student Writing

I think that the idea of writing celebrations must seem frivolous these days, when added to the list of heavy, bureaucratic alarms rung by test scores, achievement gaps, and now, national core standards, that hang over our heads. But what writers like Mem Fox and Billy Collins know is that none of that standards stuff means one lick if no one is reading and accepting your writing, and this goes quadruple for most students in classrooms.

So let's talk about that word *celebration*. It usually follows the words *birthday, graduation, anniversary*, right? The word *celebration* may conjure up images of cake, cameras flashing, balloons, champagne bubbles. Perhaps there's dancing involved, and lots of zeros following the dollar sign. But besides the party-time accoutrements, a celebration provides a formalized, ritualized way to lift up an individual and respond to his or her accomplishments.

The word *celebrate* actually means to gather in large numbers to commemorate, or to make something public and famous, to mark and to honor. Honestly, those grandiose words frighten me. When my mother turned ninety years old, I felt pressure to invent a spectacle that would properly commemorate and honor such a special birthday. What could possibly suffice? Having ideas for themes, exciting destinations, or cool decorations is not a strength for me. Many holidays and noteworthy occasions go by in my life without fanfare; I think it's because I'm terribly afraid I won't pick the best place or give enough gifts, or honor things the way they should be honored.

When I was teaching, I relied on my dear colleagues to manage all holiday parties and graduations. Give me jobs to do, I'd beg. Put me on clean-up duty; I'll do anything—just don't ask me to have ideas about things like costumes or food. Happily, celebrations don't always involve visits to the party store or consumption of big sheets of white cake with sugar icing. In the writing workshop, we can simply try to infuse more of a sense of the joy, anticipation, and caring response that gives purpose to writing, and we can do that every day in our writing conferences and share sessions by noticing and naming what each student does brilliantly in his or her writing.

We've gotten good at the *work* part of workshop! Kids generate ideas, draft, revise, and edit them for commas, paragraphs, and spelling, and then—oops! The winter break is here, benchmarks, end-of-unit tests, and state tests are here, field trip to the state history museum is here, and then it's time to start the next writing unit, and there goes the celebration part. All across the land, teachers are teaching so hard. Kids are writing so hard: unit after unit and draft after draft, memoirs and persuasive essays and how-to's and lots and lots of prompted essays. Our kids have gotten better and better at doing writing workshop. But what they might not know quite as well is *why*? Why do we fill notebooks with impressions, emotions, memories, plans, and thoughts? Why do we correct our capitals and commas? Why do we need to craft rich, focused narrative scenes and not write simply, "I went to SeaWorld on Saturday and it was fun"? *Why do we write?*

To share, that's why. To share our writing with other people. To read it to family members who instantaneously weep. To a group of kids who burst into laughter or burst into song. To invisible others on the Internet who write back to us. To our teachers, who make a copy of our poem to hang over their computers for inspiration on dark days. To celebrate.

Whole-Class Writing Celebrations

Besides the multiple times we see our student writers' gifts and name them in writing conferences; besides the times we spotlight a student's breakthrough or ask them to teach the class something about their writing process; besides the daily turning to each other to share at the end of writing workshop, our student writers also need writing celebration days that take their writing to a larger public. In Melody Zoch's bilingual fourth-grade classroom in Austin, Texas, such a writing celebration happened. Melody, the bravest fourth-grade teacher I know, who refuses to let the state writing test eat up her fabulous curriculum, took out five weeks one fall to help her kids write their memoirs and then transform them into multidimensional art projects. On celebration day, she put all her tables and chairs in a huge circle around the perimeter of the classroom and draped black mural paper over them so that the kids' art projects would pop against the black background. Melody transformed the space in that room—leaping over the functions of the ordinary school day for this writing celebration. The weather area turned into prime museum space. The math center became laden with homemade cookies and cakes donated by the kids' families. On this day, an intensity filled the room, unlike regular school days.

Melody wanted her fourth graders to know that for this day, what they *wrote* and *made* was more important than the state science and social studies curriculum. She bravely took down the testing rubric with its clunky language about mechanics and organization because on this day, families and friends would only see and celebrate her students' *art*. She wanted an audience to witness and celebrate what it *is*, and not compare it to a checklist of abstract categories that highlight what is *missing*.

The kids were crazy excited. They spent a day cleaning and getting the room ready, as if preparing for a dinner party at home with company coming. The exhibit was so crowded with siblings, cousins, kids from other classrooms, and adults alike, that Randy and I had to wait our turn to get into the room. This community became a true audience and the kids were no longer students, but *artists*.

Melody's was close to what I call a *big tent* writing celebration (more about those to follow) gorgeously produced, as she is an artist herself and has a genius for design. Let's go back to the word *celebration* to consider its quieter meanings: to honor, to mark, to make public. How can we do those things, without hiring caterers and a dance band?

Ways to Respond to Student Writing in the Classroom

Let's think of sharing in the classroom as an easy and instantaneous way to get readers' responses, not only at the end of a unit of study with a final product, but every day, as kids are composing and revising. There are hundreds of opportunities to share kids' writing in minilessons, conferences, and share sessions, obviously. But here are some additional possibilities for response from my own classrooms or events that I've witnessed in classrooms across the country.

Partners and Writing Groups

I'm a huge fan of writing partners and groups, and I've used them in all my classrooms, no matter the age of the writers. I also use them when I teach writing to adults, and often the people in those groups become so close, they carry on at the end of the summer institute or college semester, meeting after school or on weekends. Many times, teachers in my writing classes have credited their peer groups with helping them write something meaningful for the first time in their lives. In the Clear Creek School District outside of Houston, Texas, I've been the luckiest person to be able to work with a group of smart and devoted literacy coaches on their own writing. We take two days to "retreat" away from school buildings to write and share in partners and in groups. The writing this group produces time after time brings the group closer together as we laugh and cry in response. We all fall madly in love with each other through our shared writing. Molly McClure summed it up for us: "This is so powerful. Hearing how everyone's writing connects with their lives and how we are learning from each other. We're even lifting lines from each other's writing to weave into our own writing."

While we may not be able to retreat somewhere with our students, we can re-create the power of sharing writing in partnerships and small groups in our own classrooms. At all stages of the writing process, from getting ideas to finding information resources to playing out different structures to reading parts out loud for help with the music, peer readers can be the best motivators for writing and revising.

My friend, Deb Kelt, teaches ninth grade in Austin, Texas. I am privileged to be able to visit her class to watch this deeply caring, exceedingly smart teacher in action. One day, I went to her class to do a minilesson and confer with her ninth graders about revising poems. Deb had sent me some draft poems to look at before I came, and one poem, called "My Little Sister's Little Pink Purse," particularly caught my eye. I told Deb in an email that I especially wanted to confer with Ramone, the poet.

"Oh, Ramone!" Deb wrote back. "He is such a tough kid. He comes to school maybe three days a week, and when he shows up, he rarely writes or reads anything. This poem about his little sister was a revelation! He wrote it in about ten minutes!"

My Little Sister's Little Pink Purse

It's a little pink purse. She
takes it everywhere like Walmart
Sometimes she acts like she is
gonna pay with money she thinks she
has in that little pink purse.
I hope she keeps on with that little
pink purse. I hope she achives & does
the right things with that little pink purse.
Sometimes I worry if she
will let go of that little pink purse.

Deb promised to call his house and lure him to class, telling him that this "famous poet lady" wanted to talk to him. Ramone did not show up the day I intended to celebrate him. Kids in class sent him text messages on their cell phones, and then Deb even said, "Yeah, go ahead and call him!" Yazmeen called first and said, "Miss! Ramone's in the gym!" But he refused to come up and join us. When I asked kids to share what they were working on with their partners, Ramone's partner, Manuel, wrote him a note to give to Ramone whenever he decided to show up again. Manuel wrote: "I like dat Ramone talks about his lil sister and her pink purse. The purse is like her guardian. Like a blind man's dog."

Manuel's response to his friend's brilliance is a poem in itself! Teachers often worry that kids don't know what to say to each other when they read or hear each other's writing; their comments are either empty praise, "I like it all!" or they fall back on scripts they've heard somewhere: "Where did you get your idea for this story?" These are common problems when there has not yet been enough consistent demonstration and practice for how to offer effective response. When kids work in writing partnerships and groups as often as possible, they can develop the same kind of language that I talk about in Chapters 4 and 5 because they will hear it from you about their own writing and can then turn and say it to someone else.

Make Writing Public, Simply and Authentically

In addition to sharing kids' writing inside the writing community of the classroom, we can make writing public, that is, send it outside of the classroom, without a lot of fanfare, for instance by writing another class or sending notes to the school secretary, custodians, or principal. Kids can write letters to the mayor, to a presidential candidate, to the managers of video game companies. In fact, when kids produce email messages and snail-mail letters for real reasons—to protest or complain, to ask for information or permission—and not as a whole-class assignment to learn, for instance, the format of a business letter, they have the possibility of instant response that feels important because it belongs to the world, a lesson that can carry more weight than much of our writing instruction.

We can hang writing on the walls all over the school, in the gym and the cafeteria, and broadcast on the intercom system or in school radio and video labs. We can make books and anthologies, newsletters and literary journals. We can put writing on CDs and make DVDs of kids reading their writing out loud. These days, we can publish writing to the whole world, through email, social networking sites such as Facebook and Twitter, blogs, and websites. (Even as I write these words, someone has invented a new and world-changing opportunity for electronic publishing.) I know readers would help me grow this list past the covers of this book if you could tell me about the publishing and celebrations you have put together or can imagine sponsoring. But here are a few great ideas that my 2007 summer institute course participants generated with me:

- Arrange to have a student(s) watch (live or on video) two teachers, or other adults from the school building or community, read their work out loud and respond with laughter and compliments. "Really belly laugh their writing," said Stephanie Douglas.
- Put a quote from students' writing on the wall with their names under it and intersperse those with the "famous writers" quotes we're fond of hanging on the wall.

- Do a mentor author study using pieces of student writing rather than published writers. Notice the craft moves of each other's pieces and say, "I'm using that great thing Jamal does in my writing."
- Ask kids to internalize and say out loud, "I'm the kind of writer who. . . ."
- Give family members some three-inch-by-five-inch index cards to write compliments to each student as they listen to or read student writing at a celebration.
- Have a "Museum Share," setting student texts around the room, or around the building for a schoolwide museum. Invite other classrooms, administrators, and community members to attend. The audience moves through the exhibit, reading the pieces of writing in silence. Include a compliment page next to the piece for people to comment to the writer. Teach the audience members beforehand how you wish that they say only positive things in their comments.
- Hang student writing on the wall outside the classroom under a banner that reads something like "School of Writers at Work—Please Notice and Compliment Our Writing." Attach a pad of sticky notes for people to write comments and stick them next to each text. At PS 68 in Queens, New York, Andrea Evert, the literacy coach, showed me a bulletin board in her school where a teacher had written sticky notes on each of her students' pieces that read like little book reviews. All were highly complimentary, of course, drawing readers' attention to a sentence in this one and a character portrayal in that one. This is such a respectful, more specific, and fun contrast to attaching a rubric and a grade to a piece of writing, isn't it?

Some Big Tent Celebration Stories

These next few are examples of the big tent kind of celebration, and those, I admit, are the most time consuming, most difficult for me to envision. So first, here are some tips for how I, the celebration-challenged, managed to throw a few of these over the years:

- I only planned two giant, big tent parties a year. Maybe some of you can do more, and I bow to you. Of course, I offered my kids ways to take their writing to the public every single day, we just didn't bring out the candles and balloons.
- I planned backward. I put the writing celebration in first, choosing a date that worked around holidays, parent–teacher conferences, and tests. Then I planned the unit of study backward from that date.

- I asked everyone to help: my husband, Randy, the art and music teacher, family members, especially available family members. It usually wasn't hard to get help with a party. Or I shared the work and the celebration with a colleague, which makes it more fun and less work for everyone.

- I also planned two or three less intense celebrations across the year. For a memoir celebration in my fourth- and fifth-grade class, I asked kids to read their finished pieces in writing response groups of four. Then, I asked them to talk about each other's process of writing these memoirs to the family and community members who gathered around each table to listen. The response groups had been helping each other through the entire genre study, and they knew each other's work inside and out. It was unbelievably moving to hear them telling grown-ups not even related to them about their friends' strengths or about how their friends had solved kinks in various stages of the drafting and revising. We celebrated the entire process of writing, and every student's contributions to each other's work.

Celebration Stories from Other Teachers

- Shirley Gerdes, a great elementary teacher in Comal, Texas, told me that every May, each child in her school writes and illustrates a story and the school pays to publish them into hard-backed books. Then they take a whole day for a schoolwide reading of these books. This book publishing day has become locally famous over the years, and because the kids write and send out the invitations, most who have been invited, come. The mayor, the state governor, a player for the Los Angeles Lakers, and a soldier on leave from Iraq have all attended the celebration day. The Lakers player (and Shirley protectively would not divulge which one) said that when he got an invitation from a child, how could he *not* come? Absolutely!

- Kate Kuonen, a courageous and brilliant teacher in Indianapolis, Indiana, worked with her awesome fifth- and sixth-grade kids on a genre study in songwriting. Kate's students not only wrote their own lyrics, but also composed music on a computer program called Garage Band to produce a CD. But they didn't stop there—the kids were selling their CDs for five dollars apiece to raise money for their adopted family in Kenya. And in the summer of 2009, Kate went to Kenya to meet the class' adopted family, bearing more communications from her students. Her class deeply experienced writing that makes a difference in the world.

- My friend, Tasha Laman, a literacy education professor at the University of South Carolina, takes her students to writing celebrations at local elementary schools. The college kids are shocked at the quality of the writing and the enthusiasm of the young authors. They swear they will carry on writing workshop after they graduate and get their own classrooms.

- When I taught at PS 11 in New York City in the Chelsea neighborhood of Manhattan, the Sixth Avenue Barnes and Noble bookstore invited students from local schools to give readings at the bookstore. We leapt at the chance, and for several years, my students read their poetry and memoirs into a microphone in the same part of the store where famous writers came to read their work. I'll never forget the feeling of seeing strangers stop their book browsing for a little while and drape themselves over the banister from the second floor or sit around the fringes (all the chairs were taken by adoring family members, of course!) to listen to young people read their writing. Many people came up to me afterward to ask where they could get copies of this or that piece and to tell us that they did not realize kids' writing could be so beautiful and moving.

- Teachers from other cities and states have told me they took their classes to read at bookstores and coffeeshops in their towns. All it takes is a query from you to the manager or human relations director or special events coordinator, or you could ask an administrator to put in the call; I think most local businesses would be quite excited to sponsor local students sharing their writing.

Think Grand

In the end, I leave you with an image of the most amazing celebration of student writing that I have ever seen. While working in schools in Indianapolis, I witnessed the construction of this most grand event. For several years, Susan Adamson, who is the director of the Indiana Partnership for Young Writers, has been producing a thick, gorgeously designed and illustrated book of kids' writing from local schools engaged in writing workshops. Each year, a small group of local adult artists obtain one section of the anthology, and then they each make a painting inspired by the kids' poems, memoirs, and stories from that section. This year, the book was titled *Coming to Light.*

Susan papered the town with beautiful invitations depicting the artists' interpretive paintings, and at the public reading for the book, over 650 family and community members stuffed themselves into the Barnes and Noble bookstore. That was a larger group than were attending the basketball game in the gym next door . . . in Indiana!

And then, the crown jewel: Susan Adamson collaborated with Matthew Groshek, an art professor at Indiana University, to present an official exhibit of all the writing in *Coming to Light* at the Herron Museum. Mark decided to turn the design of this exhibit over to his undergraduates as their final project for the semester. The university students had only one charge, and that was to create a museum exhibit that would completely honor the kids' writing. They were inexperienced at museum design, yet they did a sensitive, gorgeous job. Everything from the choice of paint color on the walls to the placing of lights was carefully thought through. They considered where and how people's eyes would be directed. Would the messages of the writing be masked by the design elements? If so, they rejected the design. Mark was proud of how well his college students understood their charge. They elevated the children's writing in a way that convinced viewers of its authenticity and authority and did not take over with their individual design ideas.

Susan admitted to me that this collaborative museum project took a lot of time and space in her life. At one point she asked me, "And what does it get us?" Before I had a chance to answer, she thought for a moment and said, "Or should I be thinking, 'Why does it need to *get* us anything at all?' This is for the kids."

What they got was hundreds and hundreds of kids and adults who poured into this museum space where kids' writing was marked, framed, honored, literally, as *art*. I said to Susan, "Why can't schools be places where all the adults are charged with honoring kids' writing?"

In Indianapolis, I worked with a wonderful seventh-grade teacher named Marvin Snow. Marvin's eight-year-old daughter, Rachel, had written a piece about the death of the family dog, and it appeared in the book, *Coming to Light.* Over lunch in the faculty room, Marvin told me the story about the event of the dog's death from his adult, father-of-the-family point of view. He said this dog had been his for fourteen years, before his children were born, before he met his wife even, and the dog had played an integral part of his maturing, marrying, and creating a family. When it became clear that the dog needed to be put to sleep because of its various infirmities, eight-year-old Rachel was the only person in the family who could deal with the fact that this dog was going to die. On the drive to the animal hospital, Rachel sat in the backseat of the car and held the dog in her arms and talked gently to it. "She's definitely going to be a vet or something to do with animals," Marvin told me. "She loves animals and she handled the death of our dog like a pro." I could tell Marvin was about to cry all over again as he told this story. He said that she held his hand as the whole family stood around the examining table. "She was the strong one," he said.

I was moved by Marvin's narrating of the story, of how his daughter became the grown-up in the story and how Marvin made her so significant in his version. Anyone might have passed over her simple story in a batch of student writing, had it not been made important and framed as art.

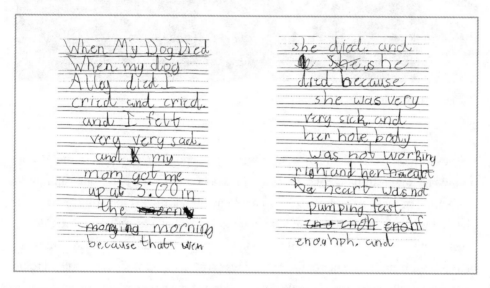

When my dog, Alley, died I cried and cried. And I felt very, very sad. And my mom got me up at 3:00 in the morning because that's when she died. And she died because she was very, very sick and her whole body was not working right and her heart was not pumping fast enough and she stopped breathing. And we had to take her to the vet so they could bury her. And I made a picture for my dog. And on Monday, I could not stop crying. And all the people in my class did not say "dog" around me. And the next day I was fine.

In all honesty, I would like to beg Rachel for that line—"all the people in the class did not say *dog* around me"—to put in one of my poems someday.

Rachel looking at her story in the museum

Susan took me to the Herron Museum after school, on our way to the airport on my last day in Indianapolis. I was anxious, as I often am when I have a flight to catch and I'm ready to go home. Susan apologized that the exhibit still wasn't completely installed, that the college kids were going to have to pull an all-nighter to finish. But when I saw it, even unfinished, with bags of installation trash waiting to be removed from the corner of the room, I was stunned and weeping, and had to be dragged away to catch my plane. When we stepped inside the room, Susan brought up the lights, and my eyes went instantly to the back wall. There, in gigantic letters cut from very thick cardboard, and lit from behind, was Rachel's story about her dog dying. It looked like a giant stained glass window in a cathedral.

We writing teachers joke, don't we—no more dead dog stories! And yet, here was one that had been literally elevated to museum-quality status and viewed by hundreds of strangers. It became art because someone declared it so.

I wish we could have gorgeous museum exhibits for every child in the world. I wish we could make every child in the world understand how it feels to have someone read his or her writing. I wish they could all know that a grown-up was comforted by an eight-year-old's story of her dog, or that someone could create gorgeous *art* in response to kids' writing. That everyone in the world could learn something about a different culture or language from children's writing, or that everyone might witness the life stories and perspectives of children who are just coming to light.

General Protocol for Reading
Published Texts

1. Respond initially to what this text says to you—what it reminds you of from your own life; what it makes you think about; what surprises you and pleases you aesthetically.

2. Point to places where you think the writing is "good." A place that stuns you—one that you almost wish you had written yourself. If possible, mark those places with circles, underlines, stars, margin notes, or use sticky notes if you can't physically mark the text.

3. Describe simply and plainly (don't label with literary terms) what the writer is doing. Even if you struggle to figure out exactly how to name this technique, describing the text will help you dig into writing craft better than slapping a label on it. You may write about how that part affects you as a reader. Push yourself to let go of all those terms you learned in school, like *simile* and *alliteration*, and try to name what the effect of that comparison or sound has on you. For instance, instead of "it's *sequenced*," try something like "I can follow the character minute-by-minute as the events unfold—as if I'm with her walking along that strip of beach, waiting for news of how the hunt went and if anyone was hurt."

4. List your responses, or fill out charts with the groups' ideas that you can then take to your own classroom to use as *cheat sheets* for responding to your student's writing. You can decide to simply list a bit of text you admire in one column and how you think the author did that in the second column. Or you can use charts such as the ones you see filled out in Chapter 3 to focus yourself on one of the qualities of good writing that often appear on writing rubrics, such as Voice and Structure (see Appendix B). (See Chapter 4 for more ideas about how to crack open the rubric labels in order to describe the qualities of writing more specifically to your students.)

Looking Closely at Qualities of Writing: Four Possibilities

Looking at *Voice* in Published Texts

What Kind of Voice?	How Did Author *Do* That?

Looking at *Structure* in Published Texts

What Kind of Structure?	How Did Author *Do* That?

Looking at *Word Choice* and *Language* in Published Texts

What Kind of Words and Language?	How Did Author *Do* That?

You can create your own lens to notice any quality of writing you wish. Depending on the text, you might consider things like details, character, beginnings, endings, suspense, line breaks (in poems), visual features (in nonfiction, graphic novels, and online texts).

Looking at _____ in Published Texts

What Kind of _____?	How Did Author *Do* That?

Looking at Whole-Class Writing

Class: _____ Genre or Unit of Study: _____ Date: _____

Research and Name

Going Well

Questions for Class

Decide

Writing Areas to Grow

Spelling, Grammar, Punctuation Concerns

Teach

Next Minilesson

What:

How:

In Future

D

Looking at Individual Student Writing

Name: _____ Genre or Unit of Study: _____ Date: _____

Research and Name	
Going Well	**Questions for Author**

Decide	
Writing Areas to Grow	**Spelling, Grammar, Punctuation Concerns**

Teach	
Next Conference	**In Future**
What:	
How:	

Looking at Whole-Class Writing
(Variation)

Student Name: _____ Date: _____

Unit of Study: _____

Initial Thoughts (A parking lot for things that immediately occur to you)

Lens: _____ (e.g., voice, structure, specific genre features. Remember to change your stance toward the positive.)

New Language to Name What I See (from ideas in Chapters 4 and 5)

New Directions to Take (What to teach the class as *writers* rather than surface features of the writing.)

1.

2.

3.

Looking at Individual Student Writing
(Variation)

Student Name: _____ Date: _____

Unit of Study: _____

Initial Thoughts (A parking lot for things that immediately occur to you)

Lens: _____ (e.g., voice, structure, specific genre features. Remember to change your stance toward the positive.)

New Language to Name What I See (from ideas in Chapters 4 and 5)

New Directions to Take (What to teach the student as a *writer* rather than surface features of the writing.)
1.

2.

3.

Detailed Protocol for Reading Whole-Class or Individual Student Writing

1. Skim across a batch of writing from your whole class. It might be everyone's writer's notebooks or writing folders, complete with drafts, or everyone's final pieces, or benchmark assessment pieces.

2. Use the templates provided in Appendixes C and D. These templates contain labeled boxes that can provide a full portrait of a whole class' or an individual student's writing progress, including places to park concerns, questions, and ideas for what to teach the class or student next.

3. For ten full minutes, look for responses to put *only* into the box labeled "Going Well." (For some teachers with generous spirits and/or knowledge of what to call the things they admired, the "Going Well" box was too small, so you may want to reshape your own worksheet or template!)

4. For five minutes, group members share out a sentence or two, or a line or two that they admire from the writing pieces. Belt these lines out with full, appreciative voices.

5. For five or ten minutes, share out and discuss items teachers find as they look through the lens of what is going well for their student writers. Make this language public on charts or document camera projections because this helps "grow" what is possible to say for the whole group.

6. For another ten minutes, teachers can work alone or with a partner to fill in the other boxes on the template.

7. For the next five to ten minutes, teachers can again share out and discuss things they are finding to put in the other boxes in the template.

Looking for the Good Stuff
in Your Partner's Writing

1. Tell your partner, the writer, what his or her piece makes you think about, what it makes you feel, or what it reminds you of from your own life. In other words, what were you thinking while you read it?

2. Point to places where you think the writing is "good." A place that you admire—that you almost wish you had written yourself. If you are reading a *photocopy* of the original writing, you can mark those places with circles, underlines, stars, margin notes, or use sticky notes if you can't physically mark on the text.

3. Describe what you think your partner is doing in those places. Don't worry if you don't know exactly how to name it. It helps if you can describe how that part affects you as a reader. Push yourself to let go and try to name what the effect of an image, or a scary build-up of tension, or natural-sounding dialogue is for you. For instance, instead of just "it's *good*," try something like "I can see your character racing down the field, aiming for the goal. I like how you described the actions, the people shouting in the stands, and the mean look on the goalie's face. I was so worried that the boy wouldn't kick it in!"

4. Before you talk today, take a few minutes to fill in a box or two on the T-charts (Appendix B) to focus yourself on one of the qualities of good writing that we have talked about in class. If you were going to notice the Voice in your friends' writing, for instance, you can write a few quotes from your partner's piece on the left side of the chart, and on the right side, see if you can describe what kind of Voice she uses. Is it sarcastic? Sad? Does it sound like a teenager whining? Does it sound like a scared three-year old?

References

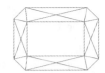

ALLISON, A. W., H. BARROWS, C. R. BLAKE, A. J. CARR, A. M. EASTMAN, AND H. M. ENGLISH JR., EDS. 1983. *The Norton Anthology of Poetry*. 3d ed. New York: W. W. Norton & Company.

ANDERSON, C. 2000. *How's It Going? A Practical Guide to Conferring with Student Writers*. Portsmouth, NH: Heinemann.

———. 2005. *Assessing Writers*. Portsmouth, NH: Heinemann.

ANSON, C. 1989. "Response Styles and Ways of Knowing." In *Writing and Response: Theory, Practice, and Research,* ed. C. Anson, 332–66. Urbana, IL: National Council of Teachers of English.

BANDY, M. 2009. "Defamiliarization." *Concrete World: 100% Skateboarding* 8(2): 57–60.

BAYLOR, B. 1986. *I'm in Charge of Celebrations*. New York: Atheneum.

BOMER, K. 2005. *Writing a Life: Teaching Memoir to Sharpen Insight, Shape Meaning—and Triumph over Tests*. Portsmouth, NH: Heinemann.

BOMER, R. 1995. *Time for Meaning: Crafting Literate Lives in Middle and High School*. Portsmouth, NH: Heinemann.

BOMER, R., AND K. BOMER. 2001. *For a Better World: Reading and Writing for Social Action*. Portsmouth, NH: Heinemann.

BRADBURY, R. 1990. *Zen in the Art of Writing: Releasing the Creative Genius Within You*. New York: Bantam Books.

BRENNER, D., D. P. PEARSON, AND L. REIF. 2007. "Thinking Through Assessment." In *Adolescent Literacy: Turning Promise into Practice*, ed. K. Beers, R. Probst, and L. Rief. Portsmouth, NH: Heinemann.

CALKINS, L. 1983. *Lessons from a Child*. Portsmouth, NH: Heinemann.

———. 1994. *The Art of Teaching Writing*. 2d ed. Portsmouth, NH: Heinemann.

CALKINS, L., A. HARTMAN, AND Z. WHITE. 2005. *One to One: The Art of Conferring with Young Writers*. Portsmouth: NH. Heinemann.

CARVER, R. 1982. *What We Talk About When We Talk About Love*. New York: Vintage Books.

DAIKER, D. 1989. "Learning to Praise." In *Writing and Response: Theory, Practice, and Research*, ed. C. Anson, 103–13. Urbana, IL: National Council of Teachers of English.

DALY, J. A., AND M. D. MILLER. 1975. "The Empirical Development of an Instrument to Measure Writing Apprehension." *Research in the Teaching of English* 9: 250–56.

DELPIT, L. 1995. *Other People's Children*. New York: New Press.

DÍAZ, J. 2007. *The Brief Wondrous Life of Oscar Wao*. New York: Riverhead Books.

DWECK, C. S. 2007. "The Perils and Promises of Praise." *Educational Leadership* 65(2): 34–39.

FITCH, J. 2006. "Oprah Talks to Janet Fitch." *The Oprah Magazine* (September): 277–80.

FLETCHER, R. 2006. *Boy Writers*. Portland, ME: Stenhouse.

FOX, M. 1993. *Radical Reflections*. New York: Harcourt Brace.

GLEIBERMAN, O. 2008. "Review of *Dark Night*." *Entertainment Weekly*, July 14. Online. EW.com.

HANSEN, J. 2001. *When Writers Read*. 2d. ed. Portsmouth, NH: Heinemann.

HEATH, S. B. 1983. *Ways with Words: Language, Life and Work in Communities and Classrooms*. Cambridge: Cambridge University Press.

HERRINGTON, A. J., AND M. CURTIS. 2000. *Persons in Process: Four Stories of Writing and Personal Development in College*. Urbana, IL: National Council of Teachers of English.

HIMLEY, M., ED., WITH P. F. CARINI. 2000. *From Another Angle: Children's Strengths and School Standards: The Prospect Center's Descriptive Review of the Child*. New York: Teachers College Press.

HOGAN, L. 2001. "Hard-Won Joy: Linda Hogan Harnesses the Power of Her Personal History." *The Oprah Magazine* (June): 121.

HUOT, B. 2002. *(Re)Articulating Writing Assessment for Teaching and Learning*. Logan, UT: Utah State University Press.

JAMES, C. 2007. *Cultural Amnesia: Necessary Memories from History and the Arts*. New York: W. W. Norton & Company.

———. 2008. "Little Low Heavens." *Poetry* 192(5): 483–92.

JOHNSON, W. 2008. *Gardening at the Dragon's Gate: At Work in the Wild and Cultivated World*. New York: Bantam Books.

JOHNSTON, P. 2004. *Choice Words: How Our Language Affects Children's Learning*. Portland, ME: Stenhouse.

JORDAN, J. 2002. *Some of Us Did Not Die: New and Selected Essays*. New York: Basic/Civitas Books.

KOHN, A. 1993. *Punished by Rewards: The Trouble with Gold Stars, Incentive Plans, A's, Praise, and Other Bribes.* Boston: Houghton Mifflin.

KÖSTER, T., AND L. ROPER. 2006. *50 Artists You Should Know.* New York: Prestel.

KUNDERA, M. [1986] 2000. *The Art of the Novel.* New York: HarperPerennial.

LYON, G. E. 1999. "Where I'm From." In *Where I'm From.* Spring, TX: Absey & Co.

MARCUS, L. 1992. *Margaret Wise Brown: Awakened By the Moon.* Boston: Beacon Press.

MCEWAN, I. 2003. *Atonement.* New York: Anchor Books.

MCLUHAN, T. C. 1971. *Touch the Earth: A Self-Portrait of Indian Existence.* New York: Promontory.

MORRISON, T. 2006. "The Reader as Artist." *The Oprah Magazine* (July): 174.

MAYER, J. S., N. LESTER, AND G. M. PRADL. 1983. *Learning to Write/Writing to Learn.* Portsmouth, NH: Boynton/Cook.

MYERS, W. D. 2001. *Bad Boy.* New York: HarperCollins.

MURRAY, D. 1982. *Learning by Teaching: Selected Articles on Writing and Teaching.* Portsmouth, NH: Boynton/Cook.

NEWKIRK. T. 1997. *The Performance of Self in Student Writing.* Portsmouth, NH: Boynton/Cook.

NOLAN, C. 1987. *Under the Eye of the Clock: The Life Story of Christopher Nolan.* New York: St. Martin's.

POGUE, D. 2008. *iPhone: The Missing Manual: The Book That Should Have Been in the Box.* Sebastopol, CA: O'Reilly Media, Inc.

POLLAN, M. 2007. "Unhappy Meals." *New York Times Magazine,* January 28. Online. www.nytimes.com/2007/01/28/magazine/28nutritionism.t.html.

PROBST, R. 1988. *Response and Analysis: Teaching Literature in Junior and Senior High School.* Portsmouth, NH: Boynton/Cook.

———. 1989. "Transactional Theory and Response to Student Writing." In *Writing and Response: Theory, Practice, and Research,* ed. C. Anson, 68–79. Urbana, IL: National Council of Teachers of English.

RAY, K. W. 1999. *Wondrous Words: Writers and Writing in the Elementary Classroom.* Urbana, IL: National Council of Teachers of English.

REYNOLDS, P. 2003. *The Dot.* Cambridge, MA: Candlewick.

SCHUSTER, E. 2003. *Breaking the Rules: Liberating Writers Through Innovative Grammar Instruction.* Portsmouth, NH: Heinemann.

SHAUGHNESSY, M. 1979. *Errors and Expectations: A Guide for the Teacher of Basic Writing.* New York: Oxford University Press.

SPANDEL, V. 2001. *Creating Writers Through 6-Trait Writing Assessment and Instruction.* New York: Addison Wesley Longman.

TATE, J. 2000. "James Tate." In *First Loves: Poets Introduce the Essential Poems That Captivated and Inspired Them,* ed. C. Ciuraru, 235–37. New York: Simon & Schuster.

THORPE, D. n.d. Amazon.com review by Doug Thorpe of *The Making of a Poem* by Strand and Boland [(2001)]. Online. www.amazon.com/Making-Poem-Norton-Anthology-Poetic.

TUNSTALL, T. 2008. *Note by Note: A Celebration of the Piano Lesson.* New York: Simon & Schuster.

UELAND, B. [1938] 1987. *If You Want to Write: A Book About Art, Independence and Spirit.* Saint Paul, MN: Graywolf.

WALL, S. V., AND G. A. HULL. 1989. "The Semantics of Error: What Do Teachers Know?" In *Writing and Response: Theory, Practice, and Research,* ed. C. Anson, 261–92. Urbana, IL: National Council of Teachers of English.

WILSON, M. 2006. *Rethinking Rubrics in Writing Assessment.* Portsmouth, NH: Heinemann.

YAGODA, B. 2004. *The Sound on the Page: Great Writers Talk About Style and Voice in Writing.* New York: HarperCollins.

ZEMELMAN, S., AND H. DANIELS. 1988. *A Community of Writers: Teaching Writing in the Junior and Senior High School.* Portsmouth, NH: Heinemann.

Index

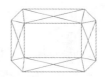

Join Katherine Bomer
for the book of a writing lifetime

Gr. 3–8 / 978-0-325-00646-8 / 224pp

PRAISE FOR KATHERINE BOMER
AND *Writing a Life*

This depth of attention to a single genre is unprecedented in books on the teaching of writing. Until now, for this depth, teachers used books written for aspiring writers and translated them into sensible classroom practice. Katherine brings writing and teaching together exquisitely in this beautiful book.

—**Katie Wood Ray**
Author of *About the Authors*

Smart teachers will read this book. Smarter teachers will use it as a guide. The smartest ones will read it, use it, and then return to it for inspiration, reflection, and, ultimately, for hope. In Writing a Life, *Bomer takes us beyond the craft of writing memoir to the purpose and passion of this genre.*

—**Kylene Beers**
Author of *When Kids Can't Read—What Teachers Can Do*

Writing a Life *has become my new "Best-book-in the-whole world." Like a best friend, this book understands what I need without my naming it, and responds in ways that are as deep and as pure as the human spirit.*

—**Lucy Calkins**
Author of *Units of Study for Primary Writing*

" There are reasons for teaching any kind of writing—to help students pass tests and progress mechanistically through the grades to college and career—that have to do with schooling and not with education. My goal as a teacher is nothing less than to change lives, nothing less than a desire to create a better world. Memoir is one of the tools I use to do that. How can a piece of personal writing accomplish such revolutionary feats? I hope that will become more evident after we journey through this book together. "

—Katherine Bomer

Writing a Life presents strategies for tapping memoir's power. Katherine Bomer shares dozens of ideas for minilessons, conferences, writing activities, prompts, and revision strategies as well as a unit on writing tests that helps students transfer the content and skills they develop writing memoir to the demands of standardized assessments.

CONTENTS:

VISIT **heinemann.com** FOR SAMPLE CHAPTERS, PODCASTS, AND MORE.

Heinemann

DEDICATED TO TEACHERS